The Dilemma of Regional Policy

Stilianos Alexiadis

The Dilemma of Regional Policy

Increasing 'Efficiency' or Improving 'Equity'?

palgrave
macmillan

Stilianos Alexiadis
Department of Strategic Planning of Rural
Development, Evaluation & Documentation
Greek Ministry of Rural Development and Food
Athens, Greece

ISBN 978-3-319-68899-2 ISBN 978-3-319-68900-5 (eBook)
https://doi.org/10.1007/978-3-319-68900-5

Library of Congress Control Number: 2017958857

Printed on acid-free paper

This Palgrave Pivot imprint is published by Springer Nature
The registered company is Springer International Publishing AG
The registered company address is: Gewerbestrasse 11, 6330 Cham, Switzerland

New Wines and Old Bottles: A Prefatory Footnote

Science is an expedition to largely unknown territories, and scientific research is a programmed action to discover new things or to develop new perspectives on existing things. One of the permanent policy and research concerns in macroeconomics and regional economics is the well-known dilemma between two fundamentally different policy objectives, namely, the maximisation of economic efficiency through a proper choice and use of resources so as to achieve a desired output and an achievement of a balanced distribution of relevant welfare components (e.g. income, growth, access to public amenities, etc.) so as to achieve an acceptable level of equity in a region or nation ('iustitiadistributiva'). The conventional interpretation of this dilemma is that we are faced with a zero-sum game: more of the one goal implies less of the other. Consequently, economic policy is a search for a compromise between conflicting objectives.

The above dilemma has induced an extant literature on the principles of economic policy. This has prompted two strands of literature—one advocated by Nobel laureate Jan Tinbergen, who claimed that the strict conceptual dilemma of efficiency versus equity is in reality less pronounced, since economic policy comprises normally multiple goals, each of which may have partial implications for both efficiency and equity. Consequently, the above-mentioned hard dilemma is mitigated through the mediating forces of multiple policy objectives. This stream of literature is clearly reflected in the emerging popularity of multiple objective programming analysis for economic and regional policy.

A second strand of literature finds its origin in the fact that the standard economic policy dilemma between efficiency and equity ought to be seen also in the perspective of space and time. A strict antagonism between two objectives might be influenced and reduced by the space-time interference of a third intervening variable which may impact the two macro policy considerations of efficiency and equity in a broader space-time context. This idea goes already back to the seminal writings of another Nobel laureate, Gunnar Myrdal, who also paid attention to the growth path and the spatial dimension of economic development.

The present volume on the resolution of conflicts between economic progress and distributional benefits, written by Stilianos Alexiadis, takes its departure in the 'old' dilemma of 'increasing efficiency' versus ' improving equity' and aims to provide a new perspective, by introducing a third intervening economic variable, namely, investments. This variable functions also as an allocation instrument and—through its multiplier and accelerator mechanism—it positions economic policy not only in a more comprehensive context but introduces also space and time aspects. This merger of a Tinbergen and Myrdal approach offers a new horizon for solving or mitigating traditional economic policy dilemmas.

The author demonstrates his analytical skills by introducing and elaborating advanced programming tools for compromise policies, based on optimal control models. This new time and space perspective through an investment mediator sheds new light on policy debates and choices on complex and interactive spatial-economic systems. This volume is a welcome addition to the rich literature on economic growth policy, in particular, as it introduces novel conceptual and analytical contributions to one of the basic problems plaguing economists.

Vrije Universiteit Amsterdam
Amsterdam, The Netherlands

Peter Nijkamp

Preface

Globalisation, an increasing concern on sustainable development and the demographic change have profound implications on the spatial pattern of economic activities in all countries. As a result, governments have implemented (and continue to do so) a range of policies for regional development. Given new social and political dimensions, along with an entirely new institutional context, an increased regionalisation of development policy is required. Contemporary regional policies, however, seem to emphasise increases in the competiveness of the economy as a whole, based on the premise that 'aggregate efficiency' can be achieved only at the expense of improvements in the spatial distribution of income. In other words, a trade-off in the aims of regional policy seems almost inescapable.

The 'trade-off' in the aims of regional policy—'regional equity' versus 'aggregate efficiency' or the so-called traditional dichotomy for regional policy used to be a popular topic in the 1970s. Surprisingly, this issue is largely overlooked in the contemporary literature. The very fact that standard textbooks on regional economics devote only a few pages on this topic was the primary motivation for writing a book, which is devoted *exclusively* on the 'dilemma' of regional policy and its implications.

Applying the principles of Mathematical Programming, this study develops an alternative approach which enables policy-makers to avoid the 'Scylla' of persisting regional inequalities and the 'Charybdis' of declining growth rates for the economy as a whole.

A precisely structured conceptual framework using ideas from regional science and basic concepts of optimisation theory will be used in order to develop a decision-making method in regional policy. This method offers concrete guiding principles for the effective regional allocation of limited (scarce) resources, namely, investment. This framework is broadly applicable and of benefit to both academics and policy-makers (or administrators) with a 'problem focus' and an 'action orientation perspective', integrated in a general strategy of economic development.

Replace the terms 'problem focus' and 'action orientation perspective' with 'objective function' and 'optimality conditions', respectively, and the above statement essentially describes an *optimisation* problem. This problem can be solved by applying principles and techniques of optimal control theory: a mathematical method that enables a researcher or a policy-maker to analyse the dilemma of regional policy and formulate appropriate measures using rigorous reasoning. To be more concrete, it will be argued that a conflict in the aims of regional policy may not be in sharp opposition as might appear. In order to develop this argument, logical deductions derived from the theory of regional economic growth and the techniques of mathematical optimisation will be applied.

In general, optimisation models have a *normative* character. Such an approach describes what ought to be rather than what actually occurs. Theoretical models of normative structure are deterministic and serve as norms or standards, which enable experiences to be compared in a precise way. The method of inference is deduction as normative theory seeks to construct what is rational or optimal according to some given criterion and is derived as a logical outcome of the integration of sets of postulates. Using optimal control theory, allocation polices that enable policy-makers to overcome the conflicts in regional policy appear as a set of logically structured propositions.

This book is structured as an extended essay, setting out a viewpoint and an argument. It refers to a wide range of areas; regional/development economics, economic geography and mathematical economics can be mentioned indicatively. The reader may well ask virtually, is there not such studies already available and what can be the justification to squeeze yet another volume onto the shelves? As far as the present author is aware, nobody has adopted the approach embodied in this study. There is a reasonable hope that readers will find a view (and a potential solution) to the dilemma of regional policy that will at least be interesting; hopefully it will also be persuasive.

In defining the purpose of economic theory, John Maynard Keynes placed particular emphasis on its role as a *method rather than a doctrine*, an apparatus of the mind, a technique of thinking, which helps its possessor to draw correct conclusions. This is a major aim of this study. In this sense, the present study may cross 'academic boarders' and can be particularly helpful for policy-making. In the process of building the major argument, mathematical language will be used extensively. Nevertheless, every effort has been made to keep the presentation and discussion in simple terms. As Albert Einstein claims, everything should be made as simple as possible, but no simpler.

A final point is in order. The approach that will be developed in this study does not provide a solution to every problem in regional economics/policy. It helps the reader to draw conclusions and making decisions. It rather aims to provide a 'premise' upon which further arguments can be built and open new avenues for future research and debate. It aims to offer an alternative methodological approach, which will help policy-makers to plan/implement policies to afford new insights and constructive intervention into the processes of regional economic development.

A very special mention is to my parents Simeon and Chrisaugi and my sister Despoina. Apart from the immense gratitude I feel towards them, I would like to mention that their presence, love and encouragement were a catalyst in realising this book.

Athens, Greece
August 2017

Stilianos Alexiadis

Contents

List of Figures

List of Tables

CHAPTER 1

Setting the Overall Context

Abstract This study attempts to illustrate the theoretical desirability and practical utility to optimising the regional allocation of investment, subject to certain constraints. A major focus of this study is to develop a decision-making method that specifies regional policies that enable maximising output and minimising regional disparities simultaneously. Stated in alternative terms, this study develops an 'optimum strategy' applicable to regional policy-making and planning in such a way as to improve monitoring and evaluation of regional policy.

Keywords Regional disparities • Conflicts • Regional policy • Economic development • Policy models • Strategy

JEL Classification R10

1.1 The Scope for Optimality in Economic Growth

'Justice', or more accurately an equitable distribution of the fruits of development, is a key notion in theoretical economics and policy-making. Indeed, 'no society can surely be flourishing and happy, of which the greater part of the members are poor and miserable. It is but *equity*, besides, that they who feed, cloth and lodge the whole body of the people, *should have such a share of the produce* of their own labour as to be

S. Alexiadis, *The Dilemma of Regional Policy*,
https://doi.org/10.1007/978-3-319-68900-5_1

themselves tolerably well fed, clothed, and lodged', an argument put forward by Smith (1776, p. 88) [emphasis added]. The importance of 'equity' in theoretical economics and policy can hardly be challenged. It has been suggested, for example, that the elimination of poverty and the achievement of greater equality in income distribution should at least supplement, if not replace, aggregate growth as a target of development policies (Stewart and Streeten 1976). 'Taking it for granted that a more equal distribution of wealth is to be desired', as Marshall (1907) argues, 'how far would this justify changes in the institutions of property or limitations of free enterprise even when they would be likely to diminish the aggregate wealth?' (p. 4). This particular quotation raises a more general question with clear policy implications: the *conflict* between the aims of improving the distribution of income (equity) and increasing wealth of the economy as a whole (aggregate efficiency). When a conflict of choice arises, a move towards one objective can be attained only at the expense of moving away from other objectives. All economics, according to Winch (1971), is concerned with is 'choice' and choices in economics always involve conflicts.[1] Conflicts are not uncommon in macroeconomic analysis.[2] As macroeconomic analysis became accepted, Ford (1971) notes,

> governments were not slow to realise that it offered them useful guidelines for managing their economies in the short run at least. For they could now devise economic policies to help them achieve some diverse objectives or targets as reduction of excessive unemployment, control of inflation and the avoidance of price increases, the elimination of gold losses by balance of payments adjustment, and the mitigation or elimination of economic instability. However, they have come to realise that *certain objectives may conflict* and that they may have to compromise by "*trading off*" the level of unemployment against price increases.[3] (p. 153) [emphasis added]

A case of particular interest is the consumption-saving trade-off implied in the model by Ramsey (1928). According to this approach, the consumer's lifetime utility depends on the time path of consumption, and the aim of dynamic optimisation is to determine the time path of consumption that maximises the consumer's lifetime utility. At each point in time, the consumer faces an inter-temporal trade-off because immediate consumption reduces future consumption by lowering capital accumulation and output growth. This trade-off is linked with the idea of *optimal economic growth*.[4]

Economic growth has been seen as a solution to a variety of economic problems. Thus, for example, it is frequently argued that 'economic growth, rather than the redistribution of income or wealth, provides the only hope of alleviating or eliminating poverty' (Jones 1975, p. 2). Dissatisfaction, however, with the 'market solution' to the problem of income distribution led economists to look more closely into the character of growth paths based on an *ethically* explicit criterion function over time. Optimal growth theory, according to Dasgupta and Hagger (1971), recognises the importance of ethical judgments by formulating them explicitly in a 'social welfare function', as proposed by Arrow (1951). In the case of the policy issues which arise in connection with the growth objective, ethical judgments can hardly be avoided. More specifically, 'growth policy is inextricably bound up with the choice of a rate and pattern of *investment*' (Dasgupta and Hagger 1971, p. 364) [emphasis added].

The analysis in this study is structured upon the notion of optimality in investment activity, which, undeniably, acts as a catalyst in the process of economic growth. The existing literature employs input-output analysis or Keynesian macroeconomic models. Nevertheless, neither Leontief's multi-sectoral input-output analysis nor Keynes' aggregate theory is in- and by itself capable of providing optimal solutions to those investment problems which *involve alternatives* and *constraints* (Kurihara 1964). In several theoretical models and empirical applications, optimal investment is examined from a 'sectoral' perspective. This resulted to a variety of frameworks in which the aggregate (national) economy is of primary interest (e.g. Koopmans 1965; Bose 1968; Dasgupta 1969; Weitzman 2005). As a result most policy analysis has focused mainly on aggregate efficiency rather than equity.[5] Investment choices are themselves bound up with the question of distribution of consumption between generations and the personal distribution of income, an issue of particular significance in mainstream economic analysis (e.g. Dalton 1920; Pigou 1912, 1949). Spatial inequality is an important determinant of interpersonal income inequality. However, little theoretical work in this direction seems to have been done as yet.

Chinitz (1966) argues that certain frameworks designed for the analysis of national growth problems might 'very logically and *necessarily* want to have a significant regional component' (p. 1) [emphasis added]. Furthermore, competition is increasing between regions, rather than countries, particularly in a context of economic and social restricting stemming from the globalisation of the economy. In an environment of rapid technological change combined with market liberalisation and deregulation, investment is more mobile. Regional investment policy, consequently, can be considered as an indistinguishable element of the overall development policy. It is of critical importance, therefore, to examine the issue of optimality in regional investment activity and its implications for regional policy.

1.2 Optimality in Regional Policy

An idea which has been much bandied around by politicians and the news media is that of economic development. An explicit concern over the existing levels of economic development across the world runs through a special field in economics, termed as development economics. Krugman (1995) defines this field as 'a branch of economics concerned with explaining why some countries are so much poorer that others, and with prescribing ways for poor countries to become rich' (p. 6). Some economists consider that this is a natural outcome, or at least the global-capitalist order of things: the rich get richer and so do the poor, but without even catching up (Hurst et al. 2000). As argued by Stewart and Streeten (1976), however, policies that emphasise greater equality within low-income countries may widen the gap of incomes between rich and poor countries, while policies that aim at reducing the international gap often widen the domestic one.

Economic development refers mainly to social welfare. Differences in economic development, according to Cox (1972), connote differences in social welfare and therefore *conflict* both between nations and between *regions within a nation* (p. 349) [emphasis added].

Regional disparities often cause political and ethnic tensions, which undermine social cohesion and economic stability. The strongest argument in favour of regional policies lies in the long-run persistence and even widening of regional disparities. In the European Union (EU), for example, despite substantial expenditure, at national and community level,[6] regional disparities remain more or less unchanged (Ulltveit-Moe 2007), while in some counties they have increased, although at different rates. Moreover, it has been suggested that overall growth can be considerably lower in economies characterised by substantial regional disparities.[7] The current economic crisis has had a major impact in the EU regions reversing long-run trends on territorial cohesion.[8] As noted by Mendez and Bachtler (2015), although there has been an upturn in economic activity recently, nevertheless, the recovery was fragile, unevenly spread and will take time to impact on territorial disparities. It seems that regional policies in the EU do not appear to deliver; they had, at most, only a (limited) redistributional impact and no efficiency gains or any significant impact on reducing regional inequalities either within countries or in the EU as a whole.

It is argued that non-optimal behaviour in the decisions of individuals, firms, governments and institutions often results in the so-called spatial error. The existing level of spatial economic imbalance indicates a considerable degree of sub-optimality, especially in the decisions with respect to regional policy. Sub-optimality in regional policy-making can be ascribed mainly to the limitations of regional development theory (Stöhr and Tödtling 1977). Although there is a plethora of empirical studies investigating the effects of regional policy[9] and the relation between regional inequality and national growth,[10] there is scarcely any definite guiding principle for the efficient allocation of resources, even in a theoretical sense, as Sakashita (1967) claims, reducing the possibility of drawing lessons for regional development policies. What is missing is a growth model whose construction depends explicitly on the requirements of regional development and which can be said to have direct policy implications.

In recent years, the literature on the theory of regional economic development, a multi-dimensional process by definition, has become very extensive and its language very complex. Notwithstanding a 'quantum leap' in the theories of regional development in the last decades, there is an area where little progress has taken place: *policy intervention* (Barca et al. 2012).

Early theorists on regional growth (e.g. Hagen 1957; Hirschman 1958) held the view that regional inequality is an inevitable concomitant and condition of growth itself. This idea is in accordance with the 'convenient textbook' approach that 'inequality is good for incentives and therefore good for growth' (Aghion et al. 1999, p. 1615). The consensus that inequality is the driving force behind growth has contributed to what Fisher and Erickson (2007) have aptly called 'a half-century legacy of equity-blind growth policy' (p. 53). With few and relatively minor exceptions, regional policies continued to rely on the 1950s development theories and 'remained cut from the same cloth: supply-side strategies – or, conversely, excessive demand-side strategies – based on a sectoral rather than a territorial dimension' (Barca et al. 2012, p. 137). Combined with changes in political ideology over the last thirty years, associated with a neo-liberal economic agenda, has favoured measures to create a more flexible and dynamic business environment through (e.g. deregulation and liberalisation of markets) supply-side measures to improve innovation, while discouraging selective government intervention such as investment aid for less-developed or lagging regions. In the EU, more specifically, barrier to trade, investment and factor mobility have been reduced, and policy-makers reconsider the aims and the content of regional policy and focus on regional competitiveness rather than redistribution. This is somehow expected since the objectives of contemporary regional policies are framed in terms of maximising the contribution of all regions to national growth or competiveness or at least ensuring that no region impedes national development, a point raised by Bachtler and Raines (2003) and signifies the trade-off in the aims of regional policy.

1.3 The Trade-Off Between 'Regional Equity' and 'Aggregate Efficiency'

It has been suggested that regional policy involves measures aimed at increasing the level of economic activity in an area where unemployment is high and growth prospects poor controlling simultaneously the level of economic activity in areas of excessive growth. Much discussion of regional policy is couched in terms of securing 'a proper distribution of industry' or diverting to the less prosperous regions 'a fair share' of national economic growth (Stilwell 1972). All these terms, essentially, describe measures to combat regional disparities. The presence of regional disparities, however, is not sufficient per se to justify the existence of regional policy (Armstrong and Taylor 2000). With respect to government policies, especially those taking a regional perspective, Richardson (1973) notes that 'the equity component is important, and although this may be incorporated in a measure of effectiveness, it may be given an independent role in the system' (p. 150). Regional policy seldom has a single aim and cannot be factored out of national concerns as might appear at first glance (Leven 1985). Instead, it has been increasingly realised that regional policies must be 'formulated within policies for national economic development' (Knowles and Wareing 1992, p. 300) or as Courbis (1982) puts it 'regional policy is not neutral with respect to national development' (p. 60).

A 'broad' perspective of regional policy puts primary concern on two indistinguishable/interrelated elements or more accurately aims at 'equity' and 'efficiency'. The former can be defined in terms of distributional justice, that is, narrowing interregional disparities while the latter as stimulating growth in the economy as whole.

This 'dual' nature of regional policy and the conflicts associated with policy choices were pointed out early by economic geographers. Indicatively, Boudeville (1966) notes that

> if the objective were to maximise, in a given period, the income of each region, national growth might be slowed down to a considerable extent. National resources are always limited, regional productivities are unequal, and regional interconnections different. Investment in less productive, less well endowed regions would put a brake on the development of more productive ones. Investment in regions less closely linked with the economic core of the nation than other would make a lower impact in total growth. Conversely, it is socially unacceptable to invest in the expanding and richest regions only. Thus, every time *choice* has to be made of a set of final goods, problems of social and political welfare are bound to arise. (p. 19) [emphasis added]

Regional analysis and policy, therefore, is an area where a choice has often to be made among competing objectives and where any given objective may be pursued with any one of several alternative instruments (Richardson 1973). Here, then, arises an intriguing and vexing problem, defined by McGuire and Garn (1969) as follows: 'How is the economist to assist the policy-maker in establishing generally applicable project selection criteria, when the objectives include equity as well as more familiar efficiency aspects?' (p. 882).

Answers to such questions, frequently posed in regional economics, have varied. 'If the planner-economist-developer is to serve as the politician's helpmate and as the decision maker's technician', according to Reiner (1963), 'he must be in a position to develop *rigorous decision mechanisms* and regional analytical tools even where politicians may shy away from too explicit formulation of criteria' (p. 64) [emphasis added].

Differences in the economic development of regions are policy issues (Cox 1972). In regional economics and policy goal, conflicts are the rule, not the exception (Richardson 1973), and cannot be eliminated by ignoring them (Stilwell 1972). In particular,

> a policy of *dispersing* economic development aids both the causes of *equity* or equality between regions and *national efficiency* in terms of economic growth. Though the argument is far from proven, there seems a widespread commitment on the part of governments to dispersion policies. A major question for the geographer, therefore, is what locational policies of dispersion will best serve both the equity and the efficiency goals? (Cox, p. 349) [emphasis in the original]

There is no formula to study the trade-off between 'aggregate efficiency' and 'regional equity' (Alonso 1975). A major aim, therefore, of this study is to cover this gap in the literature following a *developmentalist* approach. In other words, this study aims to construct an *explicit policy model of economic development.* A policy model, according to Thirlwall (1994), specifies a certain set of objectives and determines the most appropriate measures to achieve those objectives within certain constraints. Clearly, this definition refers to the notion of *mathematical optimisation.* And so, it becomes of critical importance to define regional policy in such a way that is suitable to the aims of this study. Several definitions of regional policy have been put forward. Nevertheless, Friedmann (1963) offers a definition, which is of particular relevance to this study. To be more concrete, Friedmann (1963) defines regional policy as 'the achievement of that spatial structure of the national economy which, at any point in time, is *optimal* for attaining an *efficient* path of transformation' (p. 77) [emphasis added]. Essentially, Friedmann (1963) describes a (control) problem of optimisation over time. In this perspective, regional policy is called to provide solutions to the problem of optimal allocation of resources across spatial units. Given that resources are limited, at least in the short run, a suitable method to examine the problem of regional allocation of investment is *multi-objective optimisation*, a branch of mathematical programming dealing with decision-making problems with multiple and often conflicting objectives, to be optimised over a feasible set of decisions or solutions.

In this study, the problem of conflicting aims in regional policy will be examined using the principles of Optimal Control Theory (OCT). Control theory and methods are used to find the optimal set of policies over time for a deterministic or stochastic system (Kendrick 1981). While there are several methods of optimisation, OCT enables a decision-maker to specify the development goals and on a clear course of action more rationally. Moreover, using OCT it is possible to speculate confidently about the implications of different regional policies. Applying this technique to the dilemma of regional policy, inevitably, implies an extensive use of mathematical language. The language and tools of mathematics are extremely productive in the further development of economic theory (Arrow and Intriligator 1981).

1.4 Structure of the Study

Limited resources and conflicting objectives are part of a wider concern or in the words of Gardiner et al. (2011), 'a *policy choice* between the pursuit of national growth and the reduction of regional economic disparities: policy-makers may face a "trade-off" between maximising national growth or minimising regional inequalities, and seeking the latter may jeopardize the former' (p. 981) [emphasis added]. Economic development in space is accompanied by a widening of the spectrum of resources demanded. Agents try to use resources in order to attain certain aims given the various constraints and, if possible, to 'enrich not exploit' the existing resources. These considerations, inevitably, bring forward the issue of regional allocation of investment. It is of critical importance, therefore, to find an appropriate framework.

An initial approach is provided by Rahman (1963) and, subsequently, by Intriligator (1964) who examines the problem of regional allocation of investment using the methods of OCT. The approach by Intriligator (1964), supplemented by Takayama (1967) will be examined extensively in Chap. 2. These seminal chapters outline a technically sophisticated approach for regional policy, which has been strangely neglected by the regional economics profession and never received the attention it deserved. Is it worth, however, to build an argument based on an 'old' approach? According to Pen (1965) 'if we search only for what is modern, we run the risk of overlooking truths which have stood the test of time and which are more important than the passing whims of fashion' (p. 9). The models by Rahman (1963), Intriligator (1964) and Takayama (1967) seem to be underutilised as a framework for conceptualising the possibility of a trade-of between 'aggregate efficiency' and 'regional equity'. Michel et al. (1983), supplemented by Okuno and Yagi (1990), develop a mathematical model that explicitly introduces these aims into a 'trade-off' function. However, the argument is presented in such a way that makes difficult for readers with no mathematical background to grasp its implications for policy-making. Nevertheless, some brief comments on the structure of this model and its main conclusions are set out in Chap. 3. According to Michel et al. (1983), there is only one case of compatibility between 'regional equity' and 'aggregate efficiency'. In contrast to this view, several cases, which overcome the trade-off (or kept to a minimum), are detected in Chap. 4.

Chinitz (1966) argues that if economic growth is pursued in the context of a planned economy, the role of regions is fairly clear. The importance of economic planning is obvious in the context of a free market with government activity. Planning cannot be an analytically distinct method of informing and making public policies and decisions (Reade 1983). At the regional level, a major aim of planning is to promote territorial equity through a more balanced social and economic development of regions and improved competitiveness (United Nations 2008). In other words, regional economic planning attempts to develop framework policies. If the conflict between 'regional equity' and 'aggregate efficiency' is incorporated in the process of regional development, then it provides a framework for one of the most important uses of regional planning models, and it is essential for a *rational planning* (Haveman 1977). Several implications for regional planning are considered in Chap. 4.

In the concluding chapter, this study draws some answers to the trade-off between 'regional equity' and 'aggregate efficiency' along with some concrete recommendations and avenues for further research. It is hoped that this study will make a small contribution to the design and, more importantly, to the choice of future policy instruments.

Notes

1. Examples include Kuznets (1955), Daniel (1975), Boadway (1976), Marshall (1980), and Crespo (2013), to name but a few.
2. Trade-offs can be found in other fields, for example, welfare economics (Mishan 1981; Behrman and Craig 1987; Sexton 2000; Ehlers and Klaus 2007), industrial organisation (Devine 1985), administration, (Krantz and Kunreuther 2007; Wilson (2002), agriculture (Coble et al. 2007) and health economics (Bleichrodt et al. 2005; Azomahou, et al. 2015).
3. This is the well-known conflict between inflation and unemployment, pointed out by Phillips (1958). See also Phelps (1967). Several conflicts emerge between critical variables, such as employment and growth (e.g. Pack 1974; Steel and Takagi 1983; Bičáková 2014) and output and inflation (e.g. Lucas 1973; Scarfe 1979; Ball et al. 1988).

4. Most work on pure theory of optimum economic growth has consisted largely of extensions and specialisations of the Ramsey approach.
5. In this literature interest is upon the effects of government transfers on labour supply, the cost of government regulations, the deadweight loss of taxation and so on. See also Peacock and Shaw (1971), Browning and Johnson (1987), Lazarus and McCullough (2005), Loveridge and Nizalov (2007).
6. Over 1994–1999, for example, in Portugal, Greece, Ireland and Spain, cohesion countries located in the geographical periphery of the EU, structural intervention, as a portion of GDP, was 3.98%, 3.67%, 2.82% and 1.74%, respectively.
7. This gave rise to a lengthy debate which ran for almost half a century; for partial summaries, see Pinho et al. (2015).
8. In 2009–2011 an increase in income disparities was noted across the EU regions along with an increase in regional unemployment (European Commission 2014). Moreover, even if regional disparities decline when considering the EU as whole, they increase within member states. It is interesting to note, however, that the proportion of funding allocated to lagging regions has decreased. In 1989–1993, 73.2% of commitment appropriations under the Structural Funds were allocated to Objective-1 regions, which fell to 59% in 2007–2013 and 53.5% for 2014–2020 (Bachtler et al. 2013).
9. See, for example, OECD (1970), Schofield (1979), Martin (1979), Folmer (1980), Ashcroft (1982), and Nicol (1982).
10. The studies by Robinson (1976), Forbes (2000), Partridge (2005), Lessmann (2014), McGillivray and Peter (1991) and Amos (1983, 1988, 1989) can be mentioned indicatively.

References

Aghion, P., Caroli, E., & Garcia-Penalosa, C. (1999). Inequality and Economic Growth: The Perspective of the New Growth Theories. *Journal of Economic Literature, 37*(4), 1615–1660.

Alonso, W. (1975). Industrial Location and Regional Policy in Economic Development. In J. Friedmann & W. Alonso (Eds.), *Regional Policy: Reading in Theory and Applications* (pp. 64–96). Cambridge, MA: MIT Press.

Amos, O. (1983). The Relationship Between Regional Income Inequality, Personal Income Inequality and Development. *Journal of Regional Analysis and Policy, 13*(1), 1–14.

Amos, O. (1988). Unbalance Regional Growth and Regional Income Inequality in the Latter Stages of Development. *Regional Science and Urban Economics, 18*, 549–566.

Amos, O. (1989). An Inquiry into the Causes of Increasing Regional Income Inequality in the United States. *The Review of Regional Studies, 19*(2), 1–12.

Armstrong, H., & Taylor, J. (2000). *Regional Economics and Policy*. London: Allen & Unwin.

Arrow, K. (1951). *Social Choice and Individual Values*. New York: Wiley.

Arrow, K., & Intriligator, M. (Eds.). (1981). *Handbook of Mathematical Economics*. North Holland: Elsevier.

Ashcroft, B. (1982). The Measurement of the Impact of Regional Policies in Europe: A Survey and Critique. *Regional Studies, 16*(4), 287–305.

Azomahou, T., Diene, B., Diene, M., & Soete, L. (2015). Optimal Health Investment and Preference Structure. *Economic Theory, 60*(3), 521–565.

Bachtler, J., & Raines, P. (2003). *A New Paradigm of Regional Policy? Reviewing Recent Trends in Europe*. Glasgow: University of Strathclyde.

Bachtler, J., Mendez, C., & Wishlade, F. (2013). *EU Cohesion Policy and European Integration: The Dynamics of EU Budget and Regional Policy Reform*. Aldershot: Ashgate.

Ball, L., Mankiw, G., & Romer, D. (1988). The New Keynesian Economics and the Output-Inflation Trade-off. *Brookings Papers on Economic Activity, 1*, 1–65.

Barca, F., McCann, P., & Rodríguez-Pose, A. (2012). The Case for Regional Development Intervention: Place-Based Versus Place-Neutral Approaches. *Journal of Regional Science, 52*(1), 134–152.

Behrman, J., & Craig, S. (1987). The Distribution of Public Services: An Exploration of Local Governmental Preferences. *American Economic Review, 77*(1), 37–49.

Bičáková, A. (2014). The Trade-off Between Unemployment and Wage Inequality Revisited. *Oxford Economic Papers, 66*(4), 891–915.

Bleichrodt, H., Doctor, J., & Stolk, E. (2005). A Nonparametric Elicitation of Equity-Efficiency Trade-Off in Cost-Utility Analysis. *Journal of Health Economics, 24*(4), 655–678.

Boadway, R. (1976). Integrating Equity and Efficiency in Applied Welfare Economics. *Quarterly Journal of Economics, 90*(4), 541–556.

Bose, S. (1968). Optimal Growth and Investment Allocation. *Review of Economic Studies, 35*(4), 465–480.

Boudeville, J. (1966). *Problems of Regional Economic Planning*. Edinburgh: Edinburgh University.

Browning, E., & Johnson, W. (1987). The Trade-Off Between Equality and Efficiency. *Journal of Political Economy, 92*(2), 175–203.

Chinitz, B. (1966). Appropriate Goals for Regional Economic Policy. *Urban Studies, 3*(1), 1–7.

Coble, K., Dismukes, R., & Glauber, J. (2007). Private Crop Insurers and the Reinsurance Fund Allocation Decision. *American Journal of Agricultural Economics, 89*(3), 582–595.

Courbis, R. (1982). Measuring the Effects of French Regional Policy by Means of a Regional-National Model. *Regional Science and Urban Economics, 12*(2), 59–79.
Cox, K. (1972). *Man, Location and Behavior: An Introduction to Human Geography*. New York: Wiley.
Crespo, R. (2013). Two Conceptions of Economics and Maximisation. *Cambridge Journal of Economics, 37*, 759–774.
Dalton, H. (1920). The Measurement of the Inequality of Incomes. *Economic Journal, 30*(119), 348–361.
Daniel, T. (1975). A Revised Concept of Distributional Equity. *Journal of Economic Theory, 11*(1), 94–109.
Dasgupta, P. (1969). Optimal Growth When Capital Is Non-transferable. *Review of Economic Studies, 36*, 77–88.
Dasgupta, A., & Hagger, A. (1971). *The Objectives of Macro-economic Policy*. London: Macmillan.
Devine, P. (1985). The Firm. In P. Devine, N. Lee, R. Jones, & W. Tyson (Eds.), *An Introduction to Industrial Economics* (4th ed., pp. 71–133). London: George Allen & Unwin.
Ehlers, L., & Klaus, B. (2007). Consistent House Allocation. *Economic Theory, 30*, 561–574.
European Commission. (2014). *Investment for Jobs and Growth: Promoting Development and Good Governance in EU Regions and Cities, Sixth Report on Economic, Social and Territorial Cohesion*. Luxembourg: Publication Office of the European Union.
Fisher, B., & Erickson, J. (2007). Growth and Equity: Dismantling the Kaldor-Kuznets-Solow Consensus. In J. Erickson & J. Gowdy (Eds.), *Frontiers in Ecological Economics* (pp. 53–71). Northampton: Edward Elgar.
Folmer, H. (1980). Measurement of the Effects of Regional Policy Instruments. *Environment and Planning A, 12*, 1191–1202.
Forbes, K. (2000). A Reassessment of the Relationship Between Inequality and Growth. *American Economic Review, 90*(4), 869–887.
Ford, A. (1971). *Income, Spending and the Price Level*. London: Fontana/Collins.
Friedmann, J. (1963). Regional Economic Policy for Developing Areas. *Papers of the Regional Science Association, 11*, 41–61.
Gardiner, B., Martin, R., & Tayler, P. (2011). Does Spatial Agglomeration Increase National Growth? Some Evidence from Europe. *Journal of Economic Geography, 11*(1), 979–1006.
Hagen, E. (1957). The Process of Economic Development. *Economic Development and Cultural Change, 5*(3), 193–215.
Haveman, R. (1977). On Evaluating the Regional Impact of Public Policy. In E. Smith (Ed.), *Explorations in Economic Research: New Directions in Federal*

Economic Development Programs, 4(3), 429–444, National Bureau of Economic Research.
Hirschman, A. (1958). *The Strategy of Economic Development.* New Haven: Yale University Press.
Hurst, C., Thisse, J., & Vanhoudt, P. (2000). What Diagnosis for Europe's Ailing Regions? *European Investment Bank Papers, 5*(1), 9–29.
Intriligator, M. (1964). Regional Allocation of Investment: Comment. *Quarterly Journal of Economics, 78*(4), 659–662.
Jones, H. (1975). *An Introduction to Modern Theories of Economic Growth.* London: Thomas Nelson Ltd.
Kendrick, D. (1981). Control Theory with Applications to Economics. In K. Arrow & M. Intriligator (Eds.), *Handbook of Mathematical Economics* (Vol. 1, pp. 111–158). North Holland: Elsevier.
Knowles, R., & Wareing, J. (1992). *Economic and Social Geography.* London: Butterworth and Heinemann.
Koopmans, T. (1965). On the Concept of Optimal Economic Growth. In *Semaine d'Etude sur le Rôle de l'Analyse Econométrique dans la Formulation des Plans de Développement* (Vol. 1, pp. 225–287). Vatican City: Pontifical Academy of Sciences.
Krantz, D., & Kunreuther, H. (2007). Goals and Plans in Decision Making. *Judgement and Decision Making, 2*(3), 137–168.
Krugman, P. (1995). *Development, Geography and Economic Theory.* Cambridge, MA: MIT Press.
Kurihara, K. (1964). *Macroeconomic Programming.* London: Allen and Unwin.
Kuznets, S. (1955). Economic Growth and Income Inequality. *American Economic Review, 45*(1), 1–28.
Lazarus, S., & McCullough, G. (2005). The Impact of Outsourcing on Efficiency in Rural and Non-rural School Districts: The Case of Pupil Transportation in Minnesota. *Journal of Regional Analysis and Policy, 35*(1), 55–68.
Lessmann, C. (2014). Spatial Inequality and Development—Is There an Inverted-U Relationship? *Journal of Development Economics, 106*, 35–51.
Leven, C. (1985). Regional Development Analysis and Policy. *Journal of Regional Science, 25*(4), 569–592.
Loveridge, S., & Nizalov, D. (2007). Increasing the Equity and Efficiency of Tax Abatement Programs. *Journal of Regional Analysis and Policy, 37*(1), 10–14.
Lucas, R. (1973). Some International Evidence on Output-Inflation Trade-offs. *American Economic Review, 63*(3), 326–334.
Marshall, A. (1907). *Principles of Economics.* London: Macmillan.
Marshall, G. (1980). *Social Goals and Economic Perspectives.* London: Macmillan.
Martin, R. (1979). Federal Regional Development Programs and U.S. Problem Areas. *Journal of Regional Science, 19*, 157–170.

McGillivray, M., & Peter, M. (1991). Regional Income Inequality in a Developed Nation: A Cross-Sectional Study of Australian Sub-State Regions. *The Review of Regional Studies, 21*(2), 137–151.
McGuire, M., & Garn, H. (1969). The Integration of Equity and Efficiency Criteria in Public Project Selection. *Economic Journal, 79*(316), 882–893.
Mendez, C., & Bachtler, J. (2015). *Prospects for Cohesion Policy in 2014–20 and Beyond: Progress with Programming and Reflections on the Future* (European Policy Research Paper Number 14). European Policies Research Centre, University of Strathclyde.
Michel, P., Pestieau, P., & Thisse, J. (1983). Regional Allocation of Investment with Distributive Objectives. *Journal of Regional Science, 23*(2), 199–209.
Mishan, E. (1981). *Economic Efficiency and Social Welfare*. London: Allen and Unwin.
Nicol, W. (1982). Estimating the Effects of Regional Policy: A Critique of the European Experience. *Regional Studies, 16*(3), 199–210.
OECD. (1970). *The Regional Factor in Economic Development*. Paris: OECD.
Okuno, N., & Yagi, T. (1990). Public Investment and Interregional Output-Income Inequalities. *Regional Science and Urban Economics, 20*(3), 377–393.
Pack, H. (1974). The Employment Trade-Off in LDC's – A Microeconomic Approach. *Oxford Economic Papers, 26*(3), 388–404.
Partridge, M. (2005). Does Income Distribution Affect US State Economic Growth? *Journal of Regional Science, 45*(2), 363–394.
Peacock, A., & Shaw, G. (1971). Fiscal Measures to Improve Employment in Developing Countries: A Technical Note. *Public Finance, 26*(3), 409–418.
Pen, J. (1965). *Modern Economics*. London: Pelican.
Phelps, E. (1967). Phillips Curves, Expectations of Inflation and Optimal Unemployment. *Economica, 34*(135), 254–281.
Phillips, A. (1958). The Relation Between Unemployment and the Rate of Change of Money Wage Rates in the United Kingdom. *Economica, 250*(100), 283–299.
Pigou, A. (1912). *Wealth and Welfare*. London: Macmillan.
Pigou, A. (1949). *Income: An Introduction to Economics*. London: Macmillan.
Pinho, C., Varum, C., & Antunes, M. (2015). Under What Conditions Do Structural Funds Play a Significant Role in European Regional Economic Growth? Some Evidence from Recent Panel Data. *Journal of Economic Issues, 49*(3), 749–771.
Rahman, A. (1963). Regional Allocation of Investment: An Aggregate Study in the Theory of Development Programming. *Quarterly Journal of Economics, 77*(1), 26–39.
Ramsey, F. (1928). A Mathematical Theory of Saving. *Economic Journal, 38*(152), 543–559.
Reade, E. (1983). If Planning Is Anything, Maybe It Can Be Identified. *Urban Studies, 20*(2), 159–171.

Reiner, T. (1963). Organising Regional Investment Criteria. *Papers in Regional Science, 1*, 63–72.

Richardson, H. (1973). *Elements of Regional Economics.* London: Penguin.

Robinson, S. (1976). A Note on the U Hypothesis Relating Income Inequality and Economic Development. *American Economic Review, 60*(3), 437–440.

Sakashita, N. (1967). Regional Allocation of Public Investment. *Papers in Regional Science, 19*(1), 161–182.

Scarfe, B. (1979). Optimal Monetary Policy with a Trade-Off Function. *Oxford Economic Papers, 31*(1), 20–35.

Schofield, J. (1979). Macro Evaluations of the Impact of Regional Policy in Britain: A Review of Recent Research. *Urban Studies, 16*(3), 251–269.

Sexton, R. (2000). Industrialization and Consolidation in the U.S. Food Sector: Implications for Competition and Welfare. *American Journal of Agricultural Economics, 82*(5), 1087–1104.

Smith, A. (1776). *An Inquiry into the Nature and Causes of the Wealth of Nations* (1976 Reprint). Chicago: University of Chicago Press.

Steel, W., & Takagi, Y. (1983). Small Enterprise Development and the Employment-Output Trade-Off. *Oxford Economic Papers, 35*(3), 423–446.

Stewart, F., & Streeten, P. (1976). New Strategies for Development: Poverty, Income Distribution, and Growth. *Oxford Economic Papers, 28*(3), 381–405.

Stilwell, F. (1972). *Regional Economic Policy.* London: Macmillan.

Stöhr, W., & Tödtling, F. (1977). Spatial Equity-Some Antithesis to Current Regional Development Strategy. *Papers and Proceedings of Regional Science Association, 38*, 33–53.

Takayama, A. (1967). Regional Allocation of Investment: A Further Analysis. *Quarterly Journal of Economics, 81*(2), 330–336.

Thirlwall, A. (1994). *Growth and Development* (5th ed.). London: Macmillan.

Ulltveit-Moe, K. (2007). Regional Policy Design: An Analysis of Relocation, Efficiency and Equity. *European Economic Review, 51*, 1443–1467.

United Nations. (2008). *Spatial Planning: Key Instrument for Development and Effective Governance.* Geneva: United Nations.

Weitzman, M. (2005). The Bose Model and National Income. In S. Lahari & P. Maiti (Eds.), *Economic Theory in a Changing World* (pp. 17–26). Oxford: Oxford University Press.

Wilson, F. (2002). Dilemmas of Appraisal. *European Management Journal, 20*(6), 620–629.

Winch, D. (1971). *Analytical Welfare Economics.* London: Penguin.

CHAPTER 2

Regional Allocation of Investment

Abstract Economic theory can be conceived as a logical development of a closely related set of ideas. Using logical deductions, this chapter outlines a decision-making method applicable to the problem of regional allocation of investment, based on the principles of Optimal Control Theory. This chapter presents an in-depth analysis of the process by which optimisation techniques can be used to derive allocation/regional policies. Essentially this chapter provides a conceptual base for regional policy.

Keywords Optimal control • Regional allocation of investment • Optimal policies • Constraints • Allocation parameter • Switching time

JEL Classification R10

2.1 Introduction

Regional actions have an economic focus, seeking to generate or manage and guide regional development through a variety of measures. The question, then, is whether the aggregate demand for investment can be efficiently disaggregated or 'sort out' by region, leading to a system of multiple inducements depending upon the responses they are likely to bring forth.

S. Alexiadis, *The Dilemma of Regional Policy*,
https://doi.org/10.1007/978-3-319-68900-5_2

In this respect, a framework of particular importance is provided by Rahman (1963), who considers the 'scarcity-based' conception in economics. Essentially, Rahman (1963) develops a general analytic and policy framework for the optimal or 'economically efficient' allocation of resources.[1] Using an economy with two regions, characterised by variations in savings and productivity rates as a general setting, Rahman (1963) proves that it is possible to maximise total (national) output by *concentrating* investment in only one region. The choice is made based on the existing differences in the 'internal rate of growth', defined as the ratio of a region's saving rate to its capital/output ratio, that is, the increment to savings resulting from unit investment.[2] The analysis by Rahman (1963) is based upon the 'Principle of Optimality', as proposed by Bellman (1954), which states that 'whatever the initial state and initial decisions are, the remaining decisions must constitute an optimal policy with regard to the state resulting from the first decisions' (p. 504). This framework implies that there are two types of optimal programmes of regional allocation of investment. According to the first type, investment is concentrated in the more productive region, that is, the region with the higher rate of growth. The reason for this resides to the fact that the less productive region is unable to offer a rate of saving enough to offset higher productivity of the other region. Investment takes place initially in the less productive region, according to the second type, and subsequently there is switch to the more productive region, so that the initial loss of income resulting from investment in the less productive region can be recovered by the higher saving rate of this region.

Getting a little ahead of the story, Intriligator (1964) argues that the problem of regional allocation of investment can be solved by applying the principles of OCT, an argument that constitutes the 'core' of this chapter. Prior to this, however, the basic elements of OCT are set out in Sect. 2.2. The analysis will be conducted in a standard neoclassical model of regional growth, which will be outlined in Sect. 2.3. Particular emphasis is placed upon the production and investment functions from which the main criteria for optimality in the regional allocation of investment can be obtained. The process by which optimal allocation policies can be derived is examined in Sect. 2.4, while a point of particular importance, the switching time, is analysed in Sect. 2.5. Finally, a summary is provided in Sect. 2.6.

2.2 Optimality: General Principles

The main concern of economics is the study of making the best use of scarce resources.[3] This is equivalent to maximisation subject to constraints. Stating in alternative terms, the basic economic problem is allocating scarce resources among competing ends. Goal-seeking agents, organisations and policy-makers are faced, therefore, with a problem of choice in order to realise their goals. Decision-making is the process whereby alternative courses of action are evaluated and a decision made as to the appropriate action. A decision-maker, however, as globally rational economic individual is not tenable because information is not always free, and decision-makers have limited ability to process and use the information they acquire in order to formulate and solve complex problems with conflicting aims, a notion known as 'bounded rationality'. In multi-objective problems, feasible solutions are only described implicitly, through a set of *constraints* in the form of mathematical functions, which may appear as equalities and/or inequalities.

All constrained maximisation problems have a common mathematical structure,[4] which in turn generates a common economic intuition for them (Dixit 1990). A researcher has a considerable array of approaches at hand, ranging from Dynamic Programming to 'Maximum Principle'.[5] These are fully equivalent alternative methods for optimisation over time. It is argued that the former is better when time is continuous and there is no uncertainty, while the latter has an advantage in the opposite case of discrete time and uncertainty. This, however, is not a hard and fast rule. One can use whichever is simpler for tackling the particular problem at hand (Dixit 1990). Nevertheless, given that this study takes the model by Intriligator (1964) as its premise, it will be helpful to have a bird's eye view of OCT.

In a nutshell, OCT is a system that can be encapsulated in terms of a differential equation, which describes how the state variables evolve over time and is a function of time, the state variable or the target value of the system and the control variable (policy instrument). The value of the policy instrument, which is to be selected by policy-makers, is dependent upon the magnitude of the target variable and/or time. The problem of efficient choice between available alternatives involves the consideration of objectives in relation to instruments (Vietorisz 1967). Optimisation models require a specification of an operational performance criterion or an objective function which details the quantity/quantities to be maximised (or minimised) subject to certain constraints. Thus, $\max_{x} F(x)$, subject to $x \in X$, where X is a given subset of Euclidean n-space $x \subset E^n$ and $x = (x_1, x_2, \ldots, x_n)'$ is a column vector[6] of n choice variables, $F(x)$ is a given real-valued function of these variables, $F(x) = F(x_1, x_2, \ldots, x_n)$. It is generally assumed that X is not empty, that is, there exists a feasible vector x, where x is feasible if and only if $x \in X$. Alternatively, x is the vector of instruments, $F(x)$ is the 'objective' or the 'criterion' function, and the set X of feasible (policy) instruments vectors is frequently called the 'opportunity set', reflecting constraints on the instruments.

The problem of resource allocation, the main focus of this study, can be interpreted as one of mathematical programming, which according to Kurihara (1964) has the unique advantage of 'being able to indicate the best possible path to reach a certain economic target if and when there are selective feasible paths and various limitations, institutional, or political nature' (p. 83). A particular resource allocation is represented by the choice of a particular vector of instruments; the scarcity of the resources by the opportunity set and the competing ends are represented by the objective function, which gives the value attached to each of the alternative allocations. The solution to this problem is to choose instruments within the opportunity set so as to maximise the objective function. Global maximum (or solution): a vector x^* for which $x^* \in X \wedge F(x^*) \geq F(x), \forall x \in X$. This is a solution in that the instrument vector yields a value for the objective function that is no less than its value at any feasible instrument vector. Strict global maximum is a vector x^* which satisfies $x^* \in X \wedge F(x^*) > F(x)$, $\forall x \in X$ with $x \neq x^*$.

In terms of OCT, more precisely, a typical notation of the optimisation problem appears as follows:

$$\max \int_0^T F\left[\mathbf{x}(t), \mathbf{u}(t), t\right] dt \text{ subject to } dx_i / dt \equiv \dot{x}_i = Q_i\left[\mathbf{x}(t), \mathbf{u}(t), t\right];$$

$x_i(0) = x_{i,0}$; $x_i(T) \geq 0$; $\mathbf{u}(t) \in \Upsilon$, $\Upsilon \in R^m$, where $x_i(0)$ and $x_i(T)$ denote the initial conditions and the terminal conditions for each state variable, respectively. The state of the system at any point in time is described by the n-vector $\mathbf{x}(t)$, while the control (choice) variables are described by the m-vector $\mathbf{u}(t)$, $F(\cdot)$ is the time additive and twice continuously differentiable objective function. A twice continuously differentiable transition function $Q_i(\cdot)$ is assumed $\forall x_i(t)$. In order for $x^*(t) \wedge \mathbf{u}^*(t)$ to be optimal for the problem, constant λ_0 and continuous functions $L(t) = [\lambda_1(t), \ldots, \lambda_n(t)]$ are necessary.

The problem can be solved using the Hamiltonian function, defined in compact mathematical notion as $H(\mathbf{x},\mathbf{u},L,t) = \lambda_0 F(\mathbf{x},\mathbf{u},t) + \sum_{i=1}^{n} \lambda_i Q_i(\mathbf{x},\mathbf{u},t)$. Except at points of discontinuity of $\mathbf{u}^*(t)$, $\partial H(\cdot)/\partial x_i = -\dot{\lambda}_i(t)$; $\lambda_0 = 0$ or $\lambda_0 = 1$ and the following terminal conditions are satisfied: $\lambda_i(T) \geq 0$, $\lambda_i(T) x_i^*(T) = 0$. The principal rational for using OCT is to select an 'optimal control law', including the specification of its parameters, in such a way that the performance of the system is, in some manner, 'best'. A performance index which is to be maximised (or minimised) is necessary. This index represents the desired performance of the model in terms of the target variable and the instrumental variable.

Having outlined the overall mathematical context, this chapter proceeds by describing the problem of 'regional allocation of investment' using OCT. Prior to this, however, it is important to provide some elements and postulates, since, according to Vietorisz (1967) the analysis of resource allocation models depends to a significant degree on the assumptions that are built into these models.

2.3 Regional Growth and Allocation of Investment

Economic theory, is 'essentially a collection of models' (Krugman 1995, p. 27) or a 'sequence of conceptual models that seek to express in simplified form different aspects of an always more complicated reality' (Koopmans 1957, p. 142). An economic model, in turn, is 'an organised set of relationships that describe the functioning of an economic entity[...] under a set of simplifying assumptions' (United Nations 1961, p. 7). In mathematical models of economic growth, the existing 'relationships' specify how the values of different variables in the model are related to each other (Orcutt 1960). Prior to that, however, the *conceptual basis* of the problem which is to be analysed is a prerequisite for good model building (Hines 1971).

In regional economics, ideas concerning the process of regional growth, according to Chisholm (1990), are mainly derived from a more 'general economic doctrine' (p. 27), which at present is the standard neoclassical model of economic growth, as formulated by the seminal work of Solow (1956). This model is built around two interrelated equations, namely, a production function, that is, the relationship between inputs of production and output per unit in time, and a function that describes capital accumulation. Each of these interrelationships is worth considering in turn.

An aggregate production function can be written, in its most general form, as $Y(t) = F[K(t), L(t)]$. This function determines how much output (Y) is (or can be) produced at time t by a combination of the amount of good(s) which is used as capital (K) and labour employed (L) at time t. Alternatively, as Garegnani (1990) argues, this function gives the '*minimum* quantity of each factor x compatible with a given output and quantities of the other factors; it excludes, that is, all methods requiring more of x for the same quantities of factors y, z, etc' (p. 11) [emphasis in the original].

Given that capital is generally taken to mean the stock of produced means of production available to a firm or an economy at any point in time (Jones 1975), this function reflects a 'production constraint', which portrays the dependence of output on the amounts of capital and labour employed. It is a relationship with the general continuity properties of neoclassical production functions. At this point, it is important to note that the production function is assumed to remain unchanged. Stated in alternative terms, it will be assumed that technical progress is absent. Obviously, this assumption would leave any growth theorist very uncomfortable. However, it is a necessary condition, since the analysis explicitly refers to the short run. Each factor is necessary for production; a short way of expressing this condition is: $F(0, L) = F(K, 0) = F(0, 0)$ and $f(K, L) = LF(K/L, 1) = Lf(k)$, where $k = K/L$ is the capital-labour ratio, with $k \in (0, \infty)$. However, it is possible (and necessary given the concerns of this study) to reconstruct a more precise account of the nature of production in an explicit spatial context.

Imagine an economy subdivided into two regions, labelled as 1 and 2. For the sake of simplicity, a 'closed' economy and absence of trade between the two regions are assumed.[7] It is also assumed that there is one scarce factor (capital), and each region produces a homogenous output, which is proportional to the regional capital stock; in other words, the production function takes the form $Y_i = f(K_i)\ \forall i = 1, 2$. This function is concave, subject to the properties $f(K_i) > 0$ and $f'(\infty) > 0$, positive and diminishing marginal product of capital (a curvature assumption), that is, $df/dK_i > 0$ and $d^2 f / dK_i^2 > 0 \forall K_i > 0$. The general relationship can be specified further as a linear homogenous constant returns production function[8]:

$$Y_i = v_i K_i \tag{2.1}$$

In Eq. (2.1) $v_i = Y_i / K_i$ is the (fixed) capital coefficient. This is a parameter of critical importance in the process of regional allocation of investment since it reflects the productivity of capital. Capital is related to income; observe that $K_i = v_i^{-1} Y_i$ yields $dY_i = v_i dK_i$, implying $dY_i / Y_i = v_i dK_i / Y_i = dK_i / K_i$.

Growth of per capita output is mainly a function of the rate of growth of capacity, which in turn depends on the volume of resources and the efficiency of their utilisation. Increments to capacity derive from increments to resources through accumulation of capital. In other words, growth depends on various projects,[9] which when added together form total capital investment (I_i). This process can be conceived as a 'sacrifice' for immediate (current) and certain satisfaction (consumption) in exchange for a future expectation or to increase future products (Masse 1962). Alternatively, investment is a 'distribution' from the present to future. According to Shell (1968) at any instant in time, a fraction of output 'may be allocated to consumption and the remaining fraction allocated to investment in capital accumulation.[10] Once invested the capital stock is bolted down in the sense that 'in itself it is not a good that is fit for consumption' (p. 1).

Capital investment is a critical and indispensable condition and plays a key role in economic development and growth.[11] Indeed, to an economist the study of economic development is in large part an investigation into the mechanics of capital formation. According to Chinitz (1966), policies intend to operate directly on investment such as depreciation allowances, investment tax credits and similar instruments aim to raise the expected rate of return on capital investment and thereby encourage a faster rate of capital accumulation. 'If investment is viewed as a tool of economic growth, and not simply as an accommodation *to* economic growth, what about the regional dimension here?' (Chinitz 1966, p. 6) [emphasis in the original]. The process of investment has some peculiarities in space. Capital, for example, is invested, for example, largely in regions where entrepreneurs make demands for capital rather than in areas which offer investment opportunities (Borts 1960). Nevertheless, it is undeniable that capital investment is a critical factor in reducing economic, social and territorial disparities.[12] Investment is the 'dynamo' of regional growth (Richardson 1978). Regional policies allocate (public) funds which release private financial flows that can be invested in production. Moreover, regional policy often includes measures that aim to ***induce*** capital (growth-enhancing) investment. Consequently, regional policy can be considered as a geographically specific form of investment policy.[13]

An addition to capital stock is investment (Hicks 1942). In the absence of depreciation and a gestation lag, the rate of fixed capital formation equals net investment (Tinbergen and Bos 1962). This can be expressed straightforward in terms of the following identity:

$$I_i \equiv \dot{K}_i \equiv \mathrm{d}K_i / \mathrm{d}t \tag{2.2}$$

The identity in Eq. (2.2) is the simplest relation conceivable to reflect capital accumulation. All savings (S_i) are spent on investment goods. Stated in alternative terms, it is assumed that total investment is to be *continually* equal to total savings, so tautologically, $I_i \equiv S_i$. This is another simple, but of fundamental importance identity, implying that current investment is financed by the savings available to the economy as a whole and absence of any net consumption of capital. Normally, investment does not cause output to decline. Since positive output is economically meaningful, that is, assuming $v_i > 0$ is equivalent to $\Upsilon_i > 0 \,\forall\, t$: a 'non-disinvestment' constraint implying $\Upsilon_i(t+1) - \Upsilon_i(t) \geq 0$.[14]

Assuming that a constant proportion of output is not consumed, the savings behaviour in each region is represented in terms of the following equation[15]:

$$S_i = s_i Y_i \tag{2.3}$$

In Eq. (2.3) $S_i/\Upsilon_i = s_i = I_i/\Upsilon_i$ is the propensity to save[16] with $0 < s_i < 1 \,\forall\, i = 1, 2$. In a two-region economy, national output and total savings are expressed as $\Upsilon_N = \Upsilon_1 + \Upsilon_2$ and $S_N = S_1 + S_2$, respectively. Using Eqs. (2.1) and (2.3), $S_N = s_1 v_1 K_1 + s_2 v_2 K_2$; provided that $I_N = \dot{K}_1 + \dot{K}_2$, then $\dot{K}_1 + \dot{K}_2 = \gamma_1 K_1 + \gamma_2 K_2$. Since $S_i = f_i(\Upsilon_i)$, γ_i can be seen as the degree of responsiveness of savings to changes in output: $\partial S_i/\partial \Upsilon_i$ or $\partial S_i/\partial K_i$. Given that $\gamma_i = S_i/K_i$, then γ_i can be interpreted as the (constant) growth rate of each region (Intriligator 1964). Since $k_i = K_i/\Upsilon_i$ entails $k_i = 1/v_i$, the higher the v_i (or the lower the k_i) and s_i, the higher the γ_i. According to the structure of the model, therefore, and all else equal, a high s_i implies more resources for investment and a faster growth rate of Υ_N.

The analysis takes place in a 'mixed' economy in which government, under an approved system of values, assists in the allocation of production factors, deals with externalities and attempts to improve the distribution of income through incentives to stimulate capital accumulation, formation of new firms and subsidies to new products and methods of production. Government also establishes general targets for the major sectors of the economy, to serve as guidelines and inducements to firms' decentralised decision-making. Implicit in this context is the assumption that government does not own any investment (capital) goods,[17] but simply acts as a 'redistributive' agent and an 'optimiser', namely, an organisation that attempts to attain the best (optimal) outcome they think possible from a specific set of actions.

Total savings, which for the purpose of this study, will be labelled as the 'fund',[18] are polled in a government agency[19] and then allocated to each region.[20] Given the assumption that government activity is limited to a redistributive process, the expression for capital accumulation is modified as $\dot{K}_i = \beta_i S_N$. In a two-region setting, $\dot{K}_1 = \beta_1 S_N$ and $\dot{K}_2 = \beta_2 S_N$, where β_1 (β_2) is the proportion of savings allocated to region 1 (2). In a 'closed' economy, $\beta_1 + \beta_2 = 1$. Define δ as the proportion of the 'fund' allocated to region 1, leaving $(1-\delta)$ as the proportion allocated to region 2. Consequently,

$$\dot{K}_1 = \delta\left(\gamma_1 K_1 + \gamma_2 K_2\right) \tag{2.4}$$

$$\dot{K}_2 = \left(1-\delta\right)\left(\gamma_1 K_1 + \gamma_2 K_2\right) \tag{2.5}$$

Equations (2.4) and (2.5), the 'resource'-'availability' constraints, describe a 'transition system'. This system, according to Alao (1977), depicts the evolution of the 'state variables', K_i at present, as a function of the 'decisions' taken at any point in time, reflected by the 'control' variable, that is, the 'allocation' (decision) parameter δ.[21]

Regional policy, according to Haveman (1977) is any 'explicit interference in the market system – neutral government process which has an impact on the actual or potential per capita income of a depressed region. Hence *any* public policy that is incremental to the market system – neutral government norm, and has the effect of altering the per capita income of a region of interest can be considered a regional development policy' (p. 431) [emphasis in the original]. Seen in this light, the parameter δ can be considered as an instrument that encapsulates regional policy. There is one additional feature that has to be mentioned before finished dealing with fundamentals. It will be assumed that capital once placed in a region cannot be shifted into the other region. This assumption is of particular importance. In fact, it is an 'allocation' constraint which can be expressed in terms of the following inequality:

$$0 \le \delta \le 1 \tag{2.6}$$

An approach based on optimal growth models discussed by the economist is useful to the extent that they stimulate decision-makers throughout the economy (e.g. central programming officials) to examine the decisions facing them in the light of the basic preference ordering set for the economy as a whole (Dasgupta and Hagger 1971).

Consider a policy-maker who has to choose between different allocations—'instrumentally rational' actions.[22] What combination of δ will be actually chosen or which allocation policy is considered as 'optimal' depends on the 'objective' (target) function. Optimality in the allocation of the fund requires that the objective function has to be maximised over a given time period-horizon. In some contexts, it may be legitimate to regard the time horizon as being 'exogenously' determined, for example, by some political agency or the government. In others, the choice of the relevant time horizon naturally appears as an essential part of the planning problem which the economist must examine.[23]

Government is called to find solutions to specific problems within a certain time period which can be termed as a pre-specified time or programming period. As argued earlier in this section, government establishes general targets. Assume, then, that government aims to maximise aggregate efficiency. In other words, the problem at hand is to find an allocation policy which maximises total output (Y_N) over a finite time horizon (or for the foreseeable future, at least), let $[0\ldots T]$. The problem is to optimise the 'terminal-objective' function,[24] which in the present context is defined as $\max_{\delta} Y_N(T)$, subject to the constraints (2.4), (2.5) and (2.6). Following the discussion in Sect. 2.2, this problem can be solved by specifying the value of $\delta \, \forall \, t \in [0\ldots T]$ or choosing a $\delta(t)$ sequence which maximises the Hamiltonian function[25]: $H = \sum p_i \dot{K}_i$, where p_i are the auxiliary (dual) variables. Setting $i = 1, 2$, then $H = p_1 \dot{K}_1 + p_2 \dot{K}_2$. Using Eqs. (2.4) and (2.5), the Hamiltonian function appears as $H = [\delta(p_1 - p_2) + p_2] (\gamma_1 K_1 + \gamma_2 K_2)$.

Of particular importance are the co-state variables (p_i), which are equivalent to Lagrange multipliers, interpreted as the 'shadow' price of capital in each region. Alternatively, in optimising (cost-minimisation) models, they can be considered as the 'demand price of investment' in each region or as defined by Kendrick (1976), a measure of the efficiency costs of the equity constraints. Shadow prices characterise the solution and demonstrate the relationships between optimality, inter-temporal efficiency and a set of inter-temporal prices which might be used to decentralise the optimum.[26] According to Newbery (1972), shadow prices have a natural interpretation, for they value the capital stock in terms of the objective function.

The time path of δ, at an initial and a terminal point in time, determines the efficient use of available resources. The optimal value of the allocation parameter specifies which region will receive the fund. Given the assumption that at each point in time the fund is invested in one region and the inequality in (2.6), the optimal value of the allocation parameter may be either $\delta^*(t)=0$ or $\delta^*(t)=1$; two distinct allocation policies derived from a typical 'bang-bang' solution, following the OCT's jargon.

If $p_1(t)>p_2(t)$, then $\delta^*(t)=1$ and $\dot{K}_2=0$, that is, region 1 receives the sum of savings available to the economy as a whole at a given time period. Conversely, $\delta^*(t)=0$ if $p_1(t)<p_2(t)$, implying $\dot{K}_1=0$. In this case optimality requires that the entire fund should be invested in region 2. The optimal sequence of δ can be obtained by applying the 'Maximum Principle'. Since the right-hand sides of Eqs. (2.4) and (2.5) are linear (and hence concave) functions of K_i and δ, the 'Maximum Principle' is also sufficient for the optimum (Mangasarian 1966).

Two further conditions are necessary for optimality: the ad-joint (first-order) and the terminal (transversality) conditions. The former conditions specify the optimal allocation of investment at $0\leq t<T$, while the terminal conditions give the optimal value of the allocation parameter at $t=T$. Dynamic optimality links the shadow price of capital at any instances in time with the shadow prices at subsequent times. A set of differential equations describing the evolution of the shadow price of capital are, therefore, necessary. The corresponding mathematical condition is $\dot{p}_i=-\partial H/\partial K_i$ or $\partial H/\partial K_i=-\dot{p}_i \forall i=1,2$, which, together with the equation for saving and the accumulation of capital, can numerically be integrated backwards from the asymptotic solution (Newbery 1990). As will be established mathematically, the ad-jointed conditions result in γ_1/γ_2, which depicts the differential in regional growth rates. Logically

speaking, then, this ratio specifies which region will receive the fund at the initial time of the planning/programming period, that is, at $0 \leq t < T$. Given the objective function, the degree of responsiveness or the elasticity of national output with respect to capital stock in each region at the terminal time, namely, at $t = T$, is specified by the terminal conditions, defined as $p_i(T) = \partial Y_N(T)/\partial K_i(T) \forall i = 1,2$. Given that $p_i(T) > 0$, then the 'rational' choice is to invest in the region with the highest implicit price of capital at $t = T$. The choice, therefore, is determined by the ratio $p_1(T)/p_2(T)$.

The remainder of this section describes a decision-making process. Broadly speaking, a rational decision occurs when a choice is made in a certain way. A decision-maker considers all of the alternatives or courses of action open to him/her and then identifies, evaluates all of the consequences which would follow from the adoption of each alternative and selects that alternative whose probable consequences are most preferable in terms of his/her goals, which at present are encapsulated by the objective function. Lemmas 1 and 2 advance the analysis by establishing the criteria optimal selection of δ, at the initial and the terminal period, respectively.

Lemma 1 If $p_i(t)$ is a decreasing function of time, then, $p_1(t) - p_2(t) = p_2(t) [(\gamma_1 - \gamma_2)/\gamma_2]$.

Proof $\because$ $\dot{p}_1 = -[\delta(p_1 - p_2) + p_2]\gamma_1$ $\wedge$ $\dot{p}_2 = -[\delta(p_1 - p_2) + p_2]\gamma_2$, an immediate corollary is that $\dot{p}_1 / \dot{p}_2 = \gamma_1 / \gamma_2$ or $(\dot{p}_1 - \dot{p}_2) = [(\gamma_1 - \gamma_2)/\gamma_2]\dot{p}_2$. In steady-state $\dot{K}_i = 0$; $\because$ $(\partial H / \partial \delta)/\partial t = (\dot{p}_1 - \dot{p}_2)(\gamma_1 K_1 + \gamma_2 K_2)$, setting $\partial H/\partial \delta = 0$ yields $[p_1(t) - p_2(t)](\gamma_1 K_1 + \gamma_2 K_2) = 0 \wedge [p_1(t) - p_2(t)](\gamma_1 K_1 + \gamma_2 K_2)$. $\therefore$ $(\dot{p}_1 - \dot{p}_2)(\gamma_1 K_1 + \gamma_2 K_2)$; $\because$ $\dot{p}_1 - \dot{p}_2 = p_1(t) - p_2(t)$, then $p_1(t) - p_2(t) = [(\gamma_1 - \gamma_2)/\gamma_2]p_2(t)$. Q.E.D.

Lemma 2 At $t = T$, $p_1(T) - p_2(T) = [(v_1 - v_2)/v_2]p_2(T)$.

Proof $\because$ $p_1(T) = v_1 \wedge p_2(T) = v_2$, then $p_1(T)/p_2(T) = v_1/v_2$; $\because$ $p_1(T) = (v_1/v_2)p_2(T)$, $\therefore$ $p_1(T) - p_2(T) = [(v_1 - v_2)/v_2]p_2(T)$. Q.E.D.

To sum up, according to Lemma 1, at $0 \leq t < T\delta^*$ depends on the growth differentials across regions, while Lemma 2 implies that at $t = T$, the optimal value of the allocation parameter is determined principally by the existing differences in capital productivity across regions. Faced with such choices, what rules might a policy-maker develop to guide his/her decisions? Alternatively, what does this framework imply for regional policy? A first attempt to establish some directions for the possible answers to these questions is undertaken in Sect. 2.4.

2.4 Optimal Allocation Policies

Resources are not unlimited and, when become scarcer, the effects of different (spatial) allocations become of particular significance (Bartels et al. 1982). As Chinitz (1966) puts it: 'You cannot very well decide *what* you are going to do without also deciding *where* you are going to do it' (p.1) [emphasis in the original]. Defining the areas, therefore, to which different regional policies should apply, is a fundamental aspect of a large development strategy (Stilwell 1972). Using a set of Propositions, structured by mathematical logic, this section attempts to portray the locational focus of policy.

Proposition 1 At $0 \leq t < T$, $\delta^*(t) = 1$ if $\gamma_1/\gamma_2 > 1$ and $\delta^*(t) = 0$ if $\gamma_1/\gamma_2 < 1$.

Proof According to Lemma 1, $\gamma_1/\gamma_2 > 1$ implies that p_1/p_2 is increasing $\forall t \in [0 \ldots T[$; hence $p_1(t) - p_2(t) > 0$; $\therefore \delta^*(t) = 1$. Similarly, $\gamma_1/\gamma_2 < 1$ implies that p_1/p_2 is decreasing $\forall t \in [0 \ldots T[$, that is, $p_1(t) - p_2(t) < 0$, $\therefore \delta^*(t) = 0$. Q.E.D.

Proposition 2 At $t = T$, $\delta^*(t) = 1$ if $v_1/v_2 > 1$ and $\delta^*(t) = 0$ if $v_1/v_2 < 1$.

Proof If $v_1/v_2 > 1$, Lemma 2 implies $p_1(T) - p_2(T) > 0$, $\therefore$ $\delta^*(t) = 1$ at $t = T$, while $v_1/v_2 < 1$ implies $p_1(T) - p_2(T) < 0$, $\therefore$ $\delta^*(t) = 0$ at $t = T$. Q.E.D.

Proposition 3 If $\gamma_1/\gamma_2 > 1 \wedge v_1/v_2 > 1$, then $\delta^*(t) = 1 \;\; \forall t \in [0 \ldots T]$.

Proof $\because \gamma_1/\gamma_2 > 1$, according to Proposition 1, $\delta^*(t) = 1 \;\; \forall t \in [0 \ldots T[$. According to Proposition 2, $v_1/v_2 > 1$ implies $\delta^*(t) = 1$ at $t = T$; $\therefore \delta^*(t) = 1 \;\; \forall t \in [0 \ldots T]$. Q.E.D.

Proposition 4 If $\gamma_1/\gamma_2 < 1 \wedge v_1/v_2 < 1$, then $\delta^*(t) = 0 \;\; \forall t \in [0 \ldots T]$.

Proof According to Proposition 1, $\delta^*(t) = 0 \forall t \in [0 \ldots T[$, if $\gamma_1/\gamma_2 < 1$. If $v_1/v_2 < 1$ Proposition 2 implies $\delta^*(t) = 0$ at $t = T$. Q.E.D.

The policy $\delta^* = 1 \forall t \in [0 \ldots T]$ implies 'concentration' of investment exclusively in region 1. This is entirely logical given that $\gamma_1 - \gamma_2 > 0$ and $v_1 - v_2 > 1$. Similarly, $\delta^* = 0 \;\forall t \in [0 \ldots T]$ implies concentration of the fund in region 2, given that $\gamma_1/\gamma_2 < 1$ and $v_1/v_2 < 1$. This 'exclusive' character of the allocation policy is in accordance with the objective function, namely, maximisation of national output. 'Distributional' policies or policies of 'dispersion of investment' (as opposed to 'concentrated' or 'continued localisation' investment policies, in Propositions 3 and 4) are also possible. Based on the structure of the model, Propositions 5 and 6 describe such policies.

Proposition 5 If $\gamma_1/\gamma_2 > 1 \wedge v_1/v_2 < 1$, then $\delta^*(t) = 1$ at $0 \le t < T \wedge \delta^*(t) = 0$ at $t = T$.

Proof According to Proposition 1, $\delta^*(t) = 1$ at $0 \le t < T$ if $\gamma_1/\gamma_2 > 1$. Proposition 2 implies that if $v_1/v_2 < 1$, then $\delta^*(t) = 0$ at $t = T$ Q.E.D.

Proposition 6 If $\gamma_1/\gamma_2 < 1 \wedge v_1/v_2 > 1$, then $\delta^*(t) = 0$ at $0 \le t < T \wedge \delta^*(t) = 1$ at $t = T$.

Proof If $\gamma_1/\gamma_2 < 1$, then according to Propositions 1 and 2 $\delta^*(t) = 0$ at $0 \le t < T$. If $v_1/v_2 > 1$, then $\delta^*(t) = 1$ at $t = T$. Q.E.D.

Propositions 5 and 6 describe the circumstances under which the parameters of the model imply a change or a 'switch' in the allocation parameter. A switch in δ, indicates 'distributional' policies, in the sense that the fund initially is allocated to region 1 (2) and subsequently in region 2 (1). It is possible, and convenient, to present the optimal allocation policies developed in this section using a table, which can be termed as 'allocation matrix': a particular helpful apparatus for policy-making. An allocation matrix presents the optimal value of the allocation parameter for each point in time according to the conditions of the system. For convenience, an allocation matrix is constructed with respect to the growth differentials combined with the disparities in capital productivity across regions.

Tables 2.1 and 2.2 present the optimal allocation policies when $\gamma_1 > \gamma_2$ and $\gamma_1 < \gamma_2$, respectively.

In order to see the implications of each allocation policy, some additional comments are necessary. For heuristic reasons, assume that $Y_i(t) = Y_i(0)e^{\gamma_i}$, $\Delta v_{1,2} \equiv v_1 - v_2 \neq 0$ and $\Delta s_{1,2} \equiv s_1 - s_2 \neq 0$. The growth rate in each region is determined by the propensity to save and the productivity of capital. It follows, therefore, that $\Delta\gamma_{1,2} \equiv \gamma_1 - \gamma_2 \neq 0$.[27] Variations in regional incomes are an inevitable feature in the spatial organisation of economic activity; a hypothesis that can be depicted as $\Delta \Upsilon_{1,2}(0) \equiv \Upsilon_1(0) - \Upsilon_2(0) \neq 0$. In addition, assume that $\Delta v_{1,2}(t) \neq 0$ and $\Delta s_{1,2}(t) \neq 0 \, \forall \, t \in [0 \ldots T]$. An immediate consequence is that $\Delta\gamma_{1,2}(t) \neq 0$. It is scarcely an exaggeration to argue that if $\Delta\gamma_{1,2} \rightarrow T$, then $\Upsilon_1(T) - \Upsilon_2(T) \neq 0$. A switch in δ takes place when $\gamma_1/\gamma_2 > 1$ and $v_1/v_2 < 1$ or $\gamma_1/\gamma_2 < 1$ and $v_1/v_2 > 1$. In other words, an inverse relation between $\Delta\gamma_{1,2}$ and $\Delta v_{1,2}$ implies a switch in δ. This is an extremely simplified 'delta' example. Despite its simplicity, however, it shows how the system sustains 'initial' or 'established' interregional income differences. The inverse relation in the main parameters of the model carries important implications for the conflict (or for the possible compatibility) in aims.

Table 2.1 Allocation matrix: $\gamma_1 > \gamma_2$

	$v_1 > v_2$	$v_1 < v_2$
$\delta^*(t)$ at $0 \leq t < T$	1	1
$\delta^*(t)$ at $t = T$	1	0

Table 2.2 Allocation matrix: $\gamma_1 < \gamma_2$

	$v_1 > v_2$	$v_1 < v_2$
$\delta^*(t)$ at $0 \leq t < T$	0	0
$\delta^*(t)$ at $t = T$	1	0

The general assumptions, considerations and criteria for optimality should be kept in mind not only in this chapter and in the next on the conflicts in regional policy but as relevant to many of the issues raised in the rest of the book. For the present purpose, though, there is another point that deserves special note: the time dimension in the process of regional allocation of investment.

Regional allocation of investment takes place within a certain time frame. When and under which circumstances the allocation parameter changes? The answer depends very much on the time horizon and the chosen spatial unit. Appropriate policies to meet the various objectives may differ considerably according to the time period to which the objective refers. Indeed, some (but not all) of the conflicts stemming from the implementation of various regional policies turn out to be a question of differing time horizons. For each of the objective, the time period and the inter-temporal value judgments have to be specified. Estimating the time at which a change in the allocation parameter takes place is of particular importance for policy-making. This constitutes the departure point for a more elaborated analysis by Takayama (1967) and will be examined in Sect. 2.5.

2.5 The Switching Time

In a critical appraisal, Rahman (1966) casts a sceptical view and claims that OCT is applicable if the switch of the allocation parameter was to occur only at $t = T$. The argument runs as follows. The Hamiltonian function associated with the problem can be written as $H = p_1(\gamma_1 K_1 + \gamma_2 K_2)$. Since $p_1(T) = v_1$ and $p_2(T) = v_2$, then $(p_1 - p_2)_T = v_1 - v_2$; if $v_1 > v_2$, then $\delta^*(t) = 1$ at $t = T$. But $\dot{p}_1 = -\partial H / \partial K_1 = -p_1\gamma_1$ and $\dot{p}_2 = -\partial H / \partial K_2 = -p_1\gamma_2$, implying $\dot{p}_1 = -p_1\gamma_1$; this is a first-order differential equation with the solution[28]: $p_1(t) = Ae^{\gamma_1 t}$, where A is an arbitrary constant. Setting $t = 0$, yields $p_1(0) = A$, while at $t = Tp_1(T) = A$; hence $p_1(t) = p_1(T)e^{\gamma_1 t}$. Given that $p_1(T) = v_1$, then $(p_1)_t = v_1 e^{\gamma_1 t_1}$, where $t_1 = T - t$. The difference $p_i(t) - p_i(T)$

can be considered as an approximation of capital utilisation. Hence, the rate of inter-temporal change of p_i can be defined as $\dot{p}_1(t)/\dot{p}_2(t)=\left[p_1(t)-p_1(T)\right]/\left[p_2(t)-p_2(T)\right]$. If $\dot{p}_2=-p_1\gamma_2$ and $(p_2)_T=v_2$, then $\left(v_1e^{\gamma_1 t}-v_1\right)/\left[p_2(t)-v_2\right]=\gamma_1/\gamma_2$. Solving for $p_2(t)$ yields

$$(p_2)_t=(\gamma_2/\gamma_1)v_1e^{\gamma_1 t_1}+v_2-\left[(v_1\gamma_2)/\gamma_1\right] \tag{2.7}$$

Subtracting $(p_1)_t$ from both sides of Eq. (2.7) yields

$$(p_1-p_2)_t=v_1e^{\gamma_1 t_1}\left[1-(\gamma_2/\gamma_1)\right]-\left[v_2-(v_1\gamma_2)/\gamma_1\right] \tag{2.8}$$

Taking into account the condition $\dot{p}_1=-p_1\gamma_1$, Eq. (2.8) is transformed as follows:

$$(p_1-p_2)_t=\left[(p_1)_t(\gamma_1-\gamma_2)+v_1\gamma_2-v_2\gamma_1\right]/\gamma_1 \tag{2.9}$$

Differentiating Eq. (2.9) with respect to t_1, one obtains

$$\mathrm{d}(p_i-p_2)_t/\mathrm{d}t_1=(p_1)_t(\gamma_1-\gamma_2)=-\mathrm{d}(p_1-p_2)_t/\mathrm{d}t \tag{2.10}$$

Rahman (1966) argues that $\gamma_2>\gamma_1$ does not imply $(p_i-p_2)_t<0$, that is, $\delta^*(t)=0\,\forall\, t<T$. As $t'=T-t$ increases, $(p_i-p_2)_t<0$ and a 'switch' in δ takes place.

From what has been said, it is clear that OCT is applicable to the problem of regional allocation of investment. Moreover, it is a method easily grasped and applied by policy-makers and is flexible enough in order to accommodate additional features. For example, it allows a policy-maker to estimate the exact time at which the allocation parameter should be changed.

At an initial point in time, let t_0, each region is equipped with a given amount of capital stock (or capacity installed), implying that current investment will add to the capacity only in future periods. It is customary and convenient to treat the initial capital stock as exogenously determined, positive and finite (Cass and Shell 1976). Thus, $K_1(t_0)=K_{1,0}>0$ and $K_2(t_0)=K_{2,0}>0$. Using the transversality conditions, it follows that

$$p_1(t)-p_2(t)=\theta p_2(t)+\rho(s_2-s_1) \tag{2.11}$$

In Eq. (2.11), $\theta=(\gamma_1-\gamma_2)/\gamma_2$ and $\rho=(v_1v_2)/\gamma_2$ Since by definition, $v_i>0$, then $\rho>0$. If $\gamma_1>\gamma_2$ and $s_2>s_1$, then $p_1>p_2$, implying $\delta^*=1$. If $s_1=s_2$, investment takes place in the more productive region, while if $v_1=v_2$ the fund should be invested in the region with the highest propensity to save. If $\gamma_1=\gamma_2$ and $s_2-s_1>0$, then $\theta=0$ and $\rho(s_2-s_1)>0$, implying $p_1>p_2$, consequently, $\delta^*=1$. If $\gamma_1>\gamma_2$ and $s_2=s_1$, then $\theta>0$, $\rho(s_2-s_1)=0$; therefore, $p_1>p_2$, and in this case, δ remains unchanged. If $\gamma_1>\gamma_2$ and $s_1>s_2$, then $p_2^*<0$. Suppose, however, that $v_1=v_2$, which implies that $p_2^*=v_2$. If $v_2>v_1$, then $p_2^*>v_2$ while if $v_2<v_1$, then $p_2^*<v_2$. But if $v_1>v_2$ and $s_1>s_2$, then $\gamma_1>\gamma_2$. Beyond $p_1=p_2^*$, $p_1>p_2$ and $\delta=1$. Within a given period $[t_0\ldots T]$, there is a point $t^*\in[t_0\ldots T]\ni p_2(t)=p_2^*$. If $t_0<t^*$, then $\delta^*(t)=1$ at $t_0\leq t<t^*$ and $\delta^*(t)=0$ at $t^*\leq t\leq T$.

Lemma 4 If $\gamma_1>\gamma_2\wedge s_1>s_2$, then $p_2^*=\left[(s_1-s_2)/(\gamma_1-\gamma_2)\right](v_1v_2)$.

Proof If $\gamma_1-\gamma_2>0\wedge s_1-s_2>0$, it follows that $\theta>0\wedge\rho(s_2-s_1)<0$. $\because$ $p_1-(1+\theta)p_2=\rho(s_2-s_1)$ and rearranging $p_1-(\gamma_1/\gamma_2)p_2=\rho(s_2-s_1)$. Setting $p_1=p_2$ yields $p_2^*=\left[(s_1-s_2)/(\gamma_1-\gamma_2)\right]v_1v_2$. Q.E.D.

Proposition 7 A switch in δ occurs at $t^*=T-(1/\gamma_2)\log[(s_1-s_2)v_1/(\gamma_1-\gamma_2)]$.

Proof $\because \dot{p}_2=-\left[\delta(p_1-p_2)+p_2\right]\gamma_2$, setting $\delta=0$, yields $\dot{p}_2=-p_2\gamma_2$. This is a differential equation with the solution $p_2(t)=Ae^{\gamma_2(T-t)}$. At $t=T$, $p_2(T)=A$ and $p_2(t)=p_2(T)e^{\gamma_2(T-t)}$; $\because p_2(T)=v_2$, $p_2(t)=v_2e^{\gamma_2(T-t)}$. Setting $p_2(t)=p_2^*$ and according to Lemma 4, $v_2e^{\gamma_2(T-t)}=\left[(s_1-s_2)/(\gamma_1-\gamma_2)\right](v_1v_2)$. Solving for t yields $t^*=T-(1/\gamma_2)\log[(s_1-s_2)v_1/(\gamma_1-\gamma_2)]$. Q.E.D.

The expression for the switching time derived in Proposition 7 enables a policy-maker to estimate the impact of the critical parameters of the model on the switching time or the degree of responsiveness of the switching time to changes in the critical parameters of the model.

2.6 Conclusion

Chisholm (1975) argues that a theory 'must be conveyed to other people and must therefore be mapped into a language—literary, numerical or symbolic—and thereby converted into a model. In this sense, model and theory may properly be regarded, if not as synonymous, then as two sides of the same coin' (p. 123).

The analysis in this chapter replicates the way by which a policy-maker follows in order to achieve a certain aim using particular allocation policies. This chapter sets up the scene for examining the dilemma of regional policy using logical deductions from a set of definitions and assumptions. In other words, the conceptual 'architecture' that is necessary for the subsequent analysis is developed in this chapter. It provides a simplified but rational picture of the real situation. Simplified, not say over-simplified, pictures of reality, according to Tinbergen (1992) 'contribute to making understood some essential features of that reality' (p. 44). Notwithstanding its simplicity, it can be used as a basis to develop a set of principles, applicable to the design of optimal regional (allocation) policies. Essentially, it is a 'framework' or as Tinbergen (1992) puts it 'a skeleton and the flesh and blood will have to be added by a lot of common sense and knowledge of details (p. 44).

However, before taking further steps, an essential and intriguing question seems to arise at this point. This refers to the proper objective of development, as put forward by Vietorisz (1967): 'Is it the advance of the country as a whole without regard to the regional distribution of this advance, or are the interests of the individual regions to be incorporated in the definition of a national goal and, if so, in what form?' (p. 44). The question is simple and straightforward; the answer less so.

The analysis in this chapter is based on the assumption that government aims to maximise national output, namely, aggregate efficiency. As argued in Chap. 1, however, regional policy also aims in improving the distribution of income across regions. The question which now arises is whether it is possible to find an allocation policy that 'satisfies' both aims. Prior to this, however, it is of critical importance to examine these aims from a more systematic perspective. Chapter 3 aims at exploring the various meanings which may be attached to the 'trade-off' notion and, in general, conflicts that characterise regional policies.

Notes

1. This model is supplemented by a sectoral extension (Dorfman 1963). Similar models were developed for transportation (e.g. Datta-Chaudhuri 1968; Domazlicky 1977).
2. This is analogous to the 'reinvestment quotient' by Galenson and Leibenstein (1955).
3. A resource is something material or abstract that can be used to satisfy some human want of deficiency, depending on its value to humans. A 'resource' is said to be scarce when 'the existing supply of it is insufficient to meet all our requirements' (Richardson 1964, p. 9).
4. Research on dynamic optimisation applied the calculus of variations that emerged in the eighteenth and nineteenth centuries. Unlike in standard calculus, where the value of a function depends on the value of the independent variable, in the calculus of variations, the value of a function depends on the form or shape of another function. See also Intriligator (1971, 1981), Roy (1971), Chiang (1992).
5. The 'Maximum Principle', developed by Pontryagin et al. (1962), is used extensively in economic applications, especially in macroeconomics (e.g. Hall and Henry 1988). The names of Arrow (1968), Dorfman (1969), Shell (1969), Arrow and Kurz (1970), and Holt et al. (1960) are particularly associated with this work. For a more detailed review, see Meditch (1963), Weintraub (1982) and Kendrick (1976).
6. The prime denotes the transpose of the row vector.
7. An ingredient in growth is the labour input. It is assumed that the labour force grows (due to an increase in population, an increase in the participation ratio) at a constant (exogenously determined) rate: $L_i = L_i(0)e^{\eta t}$, with $\eta > 0$. Interregional disparities can be attributed, at least partly, to suboptimal factor mobility across regions and industries (Barta and Casas 1972). Labour movements, however, are assumed absent in this model, an assumption that can be tolerated in the short run.
8. Essentially, this is a 'conventional' Cobb-Douglas production function, which in a generalised form appears as $Y = pA\prod_{i=0}^{n} x_i^{\beta_i}$, where Y is the monetary value of output, p the given price of output, x_i factors of production,

A and β_i are positive coefficients. More specifically, $Y_i = K_i^{\alpha} L_i^{\beta}$ with $\alpha + \beta = 1$, a condition implying constant returns. Let $\alpha = v$ and $\beta = 1 - v$, then $Y_i = K_i^{v} L_i^{1-v}$. Defining labour productivity and the capital-labour ratio as $\overline{y}_i = Y_i / L_i$ and $\overline{k}_i = K_i / L_i$, then $\overline{y}_i = \overline{k}_i^{v}$ or in logarithmic terms $\log \overline{y}_i = v \log \overline{k}_i$, an expression which is equivalent to Eq. (2.1).

9. Several kinds of investments can be identified: expansion investment (the increase on stock of fixed capital goods), replacement investment which the acquisition of new capital goods to make up the wear and tear on old capital goods, investment in inventories and so on. Nevertheless, for modelling purposes, investment is conceived as an increase in the existing capital stock, directly productive at the firm level, without any considerations for overhead or social capital.
10. This is a close relation with the view of Ramsey (1928) on optimal growth.
11. A point made by several authors (e.g. Harrod 1939, 1948; Domar 1946, 1957; Robinson 1956; Nevile 1962). The emphasis on the central role of accelerated capital accumulation can be described as 'capital fundamentalism' (Todaro and Smith 2003).
12. Investment has contributed to increasing income in the poorest regions of the EU: their GDP per capita grew from 60.5% of the EU-27 average in 2007 to 62.7% in 2010. GDP in the thirteen countries that entered the EU in or after the 2004 'enlargement wave' is expected to increase by 2.4% for each year between 2007 and 2025 (European Commission 2014). Cohesion Policy can be considered as a mechanism for 'growth-enhancing investment' supporting structural reforms and fiscal consolidation as part of the EU economic policy mix. Cohesion Policy is an important source of investment during the crisis and subsequent recovery strategies, notably in the less-developed member states, where the funds are estimated to account for over 60% of public investment.
13. Regional policy is a *strategic investment policy* targeting all EU regions and cities in order to boost their economic growth and improve people's quality of life. It is also an expression of solidarity, focusing support on the less-developed regions (European Commission 2014).
14. Assuming that in each time period a portion of the capital stock is withdrawn or that capital is subject to evaporated decay (Shell 1968), modifies Eq. (2.2) as $\dot{K}_i = I_i - \mu K_i$, where $\mu > 0$ is the rate of depreciation, a common expression in macroeconomics and growth-accounting exercises (e.g. Henderson 1964; Nordhaus 1967). Adopting this expression, however, does not change substantially the pattern of regional allocation of investment.
15. Although there are more specialised or 'sophisticated' savings functions, the linear savings function in Eq. (2.4) is remarkably fruitful in highlighting some of the relationships between saving and economic growth (Jones 1975). See also Ackley (1965), Burrows and Hitiris (1974), among others.

16. The propensity to save can be determined also through institutional settings, reflecting the values of a society.
17. Government policies frequently take the form of public expenditure, which is considered as additional input in the production function, increasing the productivity of private capital and, consequently, encouraging capital accumulation and growth. Public investment, at least partly, works as an unpaid input that increases the productivity of all other inputs. Moreover, it influences the decision of location for firms and industries while simultaneously affecting productivity and labour costs, eliminating inefficiencies and encouraging competitiveness.
18. The 'fund' may appear either as a fixed portion of national income or as a portion of savings. In the latter case, the 'fund' is expressed as $F_i = a_i S_i$. Let $a_i = f(Y_{i,0})$ with $f > 0$, then $F_i = a_i \gamma_i K_i$ and $\dot{K}_i = \delta_i F_N$, leading to identical conclusions. A similar reasoning can be applied if the 'fund' is exogenous (e.g. external aid or a grant).
19. Questions about administrative costs are interesting, but not the focus of this study.
20. This can be achieved by imposing regulations/guidelines (or restrictions) to the banking system to divert savings to a specific (predetermined) region or set of regions or by the establishment of a national investment bank with regional organisational structure, which focus upon raising and redistributing capital for the firms in the region, as advocated by Martin et al. (2015). Of course, government is not in a position of absolute authority. In open democratic societies, policies and decisions should devolve wherever possible in a collective way with local stakeholders and investors.
21. It should be noted, however, that this parameter is not an indicator of the degree of perfection of capital markets.
22. The set of different allocations can be conceived as a set of 'instrumentally rational' actions, which aim to 'allocate means for the attainment of the actor's end' (Weber 1978, pp. 24–25).
23. As explained in Chap. 4, this approach can be considered as a model of development planning. For a discussion of very similar issues, see Grandinetti et al. (1977) and Fakin (1997), among others.
24. Alternative aims can be considered, for example, maximising aggregate income utility (Casetti 1968) or per capita consumption. However, such policies might lead to a 'windfall' income for the population of a region. Generally, politicians favour policies with 'pay-offs' before the next election. In recession times or in countries with substantial regional inequalities, policies should focus on improving productivity, rather than increasing consumption. Nevertheless, the optimal allocation of investment when government aims to maximise per capita consumption is examined in the Appendix.

25. The classical calculus of variations can be replaced by Hamiltonian methods, which are able to deal with inequality constraints. This system enables to describe the laws of motion for a perfect-foresight (centrally planned or competitive) economy. See also Shell (1974, 1987), Magill (1977).
26. 'Shadow' or 'accounting' prices attempt to measure the benefits obtained or forgone by an economy for goods not subject to market forces. It is a notion commonly used in project appraisal, and as demonstrated by Newbery (1972), it is particularly useful in evaluation techniques (e.g. cost-benefit analysis) when valuing intangible items.
27. If $s_1 = s_2$ and $\gamma_1 = \gamma_2$, then this brings indeterminacy into the model.
28. The reader's interest in mathematical economics can, for instance, refer to the contributions of Allen (1938), Yamane (1963) and Lewis (1965), among others.

References

Ackley, G. (1965). *Macroeconomic Theory*. New York: Macmillan.

Alao, N. (1977). The Dynamics of Regional Growth: Some Elementary Full-Employment, Finite Horizon Models with External Influences. *Geographical Analysis, 9*(1), 64–72.

Allen, R. (1938). *Mathematical Analysis for Economists*. London: Macmillan.

Arrow, K. (1968). Application of Control Theory to Economic Growth. In *Lectures in Applied Mathematics, 12*(2), Providence Rhode Island: American Mathematical Society.

Arrow, K., & Kurz, M. (1970). *Public Investment, the Rate of Return and Optimal Fiscal Policy*. Baltimore: John Hopkins University Press.

Barta, R., & Casas, F. (1972). A Model of Regional Income Differences and Economic Growth. *Journal of Regional Analysis and Policy, 2*(1), 19–40.

Bartels, C., Nicol, W., & Duijn, J. (1982). Estimating the Impact of Regional Policy: A Review of Applied Research Methods. *Regional Science and Urban Economics, 12*(1), 3–41.

Bellman, R. (1954). The Theory of Dynamic Programming. *Bulletin of the American Mathematical Society, 60*(6), 503–515.

Borts, G. (1960). The Equalization of Returns and Regional Economic Growth. *American Economic Review, 50*(3), 319–347.

Burrows, P., & Hitiris, T. (1974). *Macroeconomic Theory: A Mathematical Introduction*. London: John Wiley.

Casetti, E. (1968). Optimal Interregional Investment Transfers. *Journal of Regional Science, 8*(1), 101–107.

Cass, D., & Shell, K. (1976). Introduction to Hamiltonian Dynamics in Economics. *Journal of Economic Theory, 12*(1), 1–10.

Chiang, A. (1992). *Elements of Dynamic Optimisation*. New York: McGraw-Hill.

Chinitz, B. (1966). Appropriate Goals for Regional Economic Policy. *Urban Studies, 3*(1), 1–7.
Chisholm, M. (1975). *Human Geography: Evolution or Revolution?* London: Penguin.
Chisholm, M. (1990). *Regions in Recession and Resurgence.* London: Allen & Unwin.
Dasgupta, A., & Hagger, A. (1971). *The Objectives of Macro-economic Policy.* London: Macmillan.
Datta-Chaudhuri, M. (1968). Optimal Allocation of Investments and Transportation in a Two-Region Economy. In K. Shell (Ed.), *Essays on the Theory of Optimal Growth* (pp. 129–140). Cambridge, MA: MIT Press.
Dixit, A. (1990). *Optimization in Economic Theory* (2nd ed.). Oxford: Oxford University Press.
Domar, E. (1946). Capital Expansion, Rate of Growth and Employment. *Econometrica, 14*(2), 137–147.
Domar, E. (1957). *Essays in the Theory of Economic Growth.* Oxford: Oxford University Press.
Domazlicky, B. (1977). A Note on the Inclusion of Transportation in Models of Regional Allocation of Investment. *Journal of Regional Science, 17*(2), 235–241.
Dorfman, R. (1963). Regional Allocation of Investment: Comment. *Quarterly Journal of Economics, 77*(1), 162–165.
Dorfman, R. (1969). An Economic Interpretation of Optimal Control Theory. *American Economic Review, 59*(5), 817–831.
European Commission. (2014). *The European Union Explained: Regional Policy.* Luxembourg: Office for Official Publications of the European Union.
Fakin, F. (1997). Investment-Decision Criteria and Resource Allocation in Transition. *Economics of Planning, 30*(1), 17–31.
Galenson, W., & Leibenstein, H. (1955). Investment Criteria, Productivity and Economic Development. *Quarterly Journal of Economics, 69*(3), 343–370.
Garegnani, P. (1990). Quantity of Capital. In J. Eatwell, M. Milgate, & P. Newman (Eds.), *Capital Theory* (pp. 1–78). London: Macmillan.
Grandinetti, L., Pezzella, F., & La Bella, A. (1977). Dynamic Modelling in Development Planning. *Applied Mathematical Modelling, 1*(7), 379–385.
Hall, S., & Henry, S. (1988). *Macroeconomic Modelling.* North Holland: Elsevier.
Harrod, R. (1939). An Essay in Dynamic Theory. *Economic Journal, 49*(193), 14–33.
Harrod, R. (1948). *Towards a Dynamic Economy.* London: Macmillan.
Haveman, R. (1977). On Evaluating the Regional Impact of Public Policy. In E. Smith (Ed.), *Explorations in Economic Research: New Directions in Federal Economic Development Programs, 4*(3), 429–444, National Bureau of Economic Research.

Henderson, J. (1964). *National Income: Statics and Dynamics*. New York: Harper & Row.

Hicks, J. (1942). *The Social Framework*. Oxford: Clarendon Press.

Hines, A. (1971). *On the Reappraisal of Keynesian Economics*. London: Martin Robertson & Company.

Holt, C., Modigliani, F., Muth, J., & Simon, H. (1960). *Planning Production, Inventories, and Work Force*. Englewood Cliffs: Prentice-Hall.

Intriligator, M. (1964). Regional Allocation of Investment: Comment. *Quarterly Journal of Economics, 78*(4), 659–662.

Intriligator, M. (1971). *Mathematical Optimisation and Economic Theory*. Englewood Cliffs: Prentice-Hall.

Intriligator, M. (1981). Mathematical Programming with Applications to Economics. In K. Arrow & M. Intriligator (Eds.), *Handbook of Mathematical Economics* (Vol. 1, pp. 52–91). North Holland: Elsevier.

Jones, H. (1975). *An Introduction to Modern Theories of Economic Growth*. London: Thomas Nelson Ltd.

Kendrick, D. (1976). Applications of Optimal Control to Macroeconomics. *Annals of Economic and Social Measurement, 5*(2), 171–190.

Koopmans, T. (1957). *Three Essays on the State of Economic Science*. New York: McGraw-Hill.

Krugman, P. (1995). *Development, Geography and Economic Theory*. Cambridge, MA: MIT Press.

Kurihara, K. (1964). *Macroeconomic Programming*. London: Allen and Unwin.

Lewis, P. (1965). *An Introduction to Mathematics for Students of Economics*. London: Macmillan.

Magill, M. (1977). Some New Results on the Local Stability of the Process of Capital Accumulation. *Journal of Economic Theory, 15*, 174–210.

Mangasarian, O. (1966). Sufficient Conditions for the Optimal Control of Nonlinear Systems. *Journal of SIAM Control, 4*(1), 139–152.

Martin, R., Pike, A., Tyler, P., & Gardiner, B. (2015). *Spatially Rebalancing the UK Economy: The Need for a New Policy Model*. London: Regional Science Association.

Masse, P. (1962). *Optimal Investment Decisions: Rules for Action and Criteria for Choice*. Englewood Cliffs: Prentice-Hall.

Meditch, J. (1963). An Introduction to the Pontryagin Maximum Principle. In C. Leondes (Ed.), *Modern Control Systems Theory*. New York: McGraw-Hill.

Nevile, J. (1962). The Mathematical Formulation of Harrod's Growth Model. *Economic Journal, 72*(286), 367–370.

Newbery, D. (1972). Public Policy in the Dual Economy. *Economic Journal, 82*, 567–590.

Newbery, D. (1990). Ramsey Model. In J. Eatwell, M. Milgate, & P. Newman (Eds.), *Capital Theory* (pp. 220–227). London: Macmillan.

Nordhaus, W. (1967). The Optimal Rate and Direction of Technical Change. In K. Shell (Ed.), *Essays on the Theory of Optimal Growth* (pp. 53–66). Cambridge, MA: MIT Press.

Orcutt, G. (1960). Simulation of Economic Systems. *American Economic Review, 50*(5), 893–907.

Pontryagin, L., Boltyanski, V., Gamkrelidze, R., & Mishchenko, E. (1962). *The Mathematical Theory of Optimal Processes* (K. Trirogoff, Trans.). New York: Inter-science Publications.

Rahman, A. (1963). Regional Allocation of Investment: An Aggregate Study in the Theory of Development Programming. *Quarterly Journal of Economics, 77*(1), 26–39.

Rahman, A. (1966). Regional Allocation of Investment: The Continuous Version. *Quarterly Journal of Economics, 80*(1), 159–160.

Ramsey, F. (1928). A Mathematical Theory of Saving. *The Economic Journal, 38*(152), 543–559.

Richardson, G. (1964). *Economic Theory.* London: Hutchinson University Library.

Richardson, H. (1978). *Regional and Urban Economics.* London: Penguin.

Robinson, J. (1956). *The Accumulation of Capital.* London: Macmillan.

Roy, B. (1971). Problems and Methods with Multiple Objective Functions. *Mathematical Programming, 1*(1), 239–266.

Shell, K. (1968). Optimal Programs of Capital Accumulation for an Economy in Which There Is Exogenous Technical Change. In K. Shell (Ed.), *Essays on the Theory of Optimal Growth* (pp. 1–30). Cambridge, MA: MIT Press.

Shell, K. (1969). Applications of Pontryagin's Maximum Principle to Economics. In H. Kuhn & G. Szagö (Eds.), *Mathematical Systems Theory and Economics.* Berlin: Springer.

Shell, K. (1974). The Theory of Hamiltonian Dynamical System and an Application to Economics. In J. Grote (Ed.), *The Theory and Application of Differential Games* (pp. 189–199). Dordrecht-Holland: Reidel Publishing Company.

Shell, K. (1987). Hamiltonians. In J. Eatwell, M. Milgate, & P. Newman (Eds.), *The New Palgrave: A Dictionary of Economics* (Vol. 2, pp. 588–590). New York: Macmillan.

Solow, R. (1956). A Contribution to the Theory of Economic Growth. *Quarterly Journal of Economics, 70*(1), 65–94.

Stilwell, F. (1972). *Regional Economic Policy.* London: Macmillan.

Takayama, A. (1967). Regional Allocation of Investment: A Further Analysis. *Quarterly Journal of Economics, 81*(2), 330–336.

Tinbergen, B. (1992). The Use of Models: Experience and Prospects. In A. Lindbeck (Ed.), *Nobel Lectures: Economics, 1969–1980* (pp. 42–50). Singapore: World Scientific Publishing Co.

Tinbergen, J., & Bos, H. (1962). *Mathematical Models of Economic Growth.* New York: McGraw-Hill.

Todaro, M., & Smith, C. (2003). *Economic Development* (8th ed.). London: Longman.

United Nations. (1961). Use of Models in Programming. *Industrialisation and Productivity, 4*, 7–17.

Vietorisz, T. (1967). Locational Choices in Planning. In M. Millikan (Ed.), *Economic Planning* (pp. 39–130). Cambridge, MA: National Bureau of Economic Research.

Weber, M. (1978). *Economy and Society* (G. Roth & C. Wittich, Eds.). Berkeley: University of California Press.

Weintraub, E. (1982). *Mathematics for Economists: An Integrated Approach*. Cambridge: Cambridge University Press.

Yamane, T. (1963). *Mathematics for Economists*. Englewood Cliffs: Prentice-Hall.

CHAPTER 3

Conflicts in Regional Policy

Abstract Using Optimal Control Theory, it is possible to obtain a set of allocation policies that allow policy-makers to maximise total output in the economy. The objective function associated with this problem is explicitly focused upon aggregate efficiency. This aim, however, does not exhaust the possibilities of all economic choices/actions. There are several other aims, which regional policies are called to give solutions. Are these aims compatible or are they contradicting each other? The limitations of the existing theoretical frameworks are identified in this chapter. Some theoretical schemes, in which compatibility in the aims of regional equity and aggregate efficiency arises as a distinct possibility, are also discussed.

Keywords Trade-off • Equity • Efficiency • Dual objective function • Policy weight

JEL Classification R10

3.1 Introduction

This chapter attempts to shed some further light on the trade-off or the conflict in the aims of regional policy. There are conflicts between the goals of individuals, conflicts between the aims of national and regional

S. Alexiadis, *The Dilemma of Regional Policy*,
https://doi.org/10.1007/978-3-319-68900-5_3

policies, contradictions between short- and long-run policies, conflicts between the aims of different regions, between sectoral and regional policies, and so forth.

Regional policy is a national government policy influencing the distribution of mainly economic resources over part or all of the national space. In the process of allocation of scarce resources to competing ends, a trade-off (or a substitution) between 'equity' and 'efficiency' is just another one of the many tough choices that economically rational individuals have to make (Osberg 1995). Why are some regions different from others in the way they utilise or invest their resources? Regional inequalities indicate that there is some degree of underutilisation of resources (e.g. hidden talents or mineral resources), which would increase aggregate efficiency.

The analysis in Chap. 2 is based on the premise that policy-makers aim to maximise total output of the economy. Maximising national income might not be entirely preferable from society. There are several other problems in which regional policies of regional economic development are called to give solutions.

Nevertheless, before going further into this topic, the first issue that has to be considered is related to the necessity of regional policy. Perhaps, this is the first conflict that arises in a spatial context. Are regional policies really necessary or replicating what the market can already provide? Section 3.2 provides some key points on that issue, supported by some examples in Sect. 3.3. The way by which allocation policies might cause conflicts is considered in more depth in Sect. 3.4, while some possible solutions are presented in Sect. 3.5. A framework that explicitly takes into account the 'trade-off' in the aims of regional policy is introduced in Sect. 3.6. Section 3.7 offers some conclusions.

3.2 The Necessity of Regional Policy

Is the unrestricted operation of the market economy compatible with the best interest of all society? If not, what are the economic and social implications? The undisturbed market system leads to efficiency only under the assumption of perfect competition. In an explicit spatial context, the sum of maximised per capita income in each region does not equal to maximised national income per capita, except in a world of perfect competition. In the conventional neoclassical model, free trade or factor mobility combined with optimal rates of regional investment should eventually lead to an efficient allocation of resources over time and a reduction in the income and growth disparities across regions. Based on the assumption that markets are more or less perfect, any differences in regional per capita income (or productivity growth) are seen as being temporary, mainly caused by the eradication of an initial interregional or intraregional misallocation of resources, or of both. 'Growth is essentially a reallocative process', as Borts and Stein (1964) have pointed out. Interregional equity follows naturally from improvements in the efficient workings of the market. Policies to remove obstacles to the workings of the market are non-controversial, resulting in optimal allocation of resources. Consequently and not surprisingly, the aim of 'regional equity' need not be considered separately from the 'overall efficiency'. Of course, a limitation of this characterisation of the policy dilemmas of 'regional equity' and 'aggregate efficiency' is that the compatibility of these two policy aims is heavily dependent on the accuracy of the neoclassical models of interregional growth and trade. The undisturbed market system, however, leads to efficiency only under the assumption of perfect competition, but competition is far from perfect. In regional economics perfect competition cannot be assumed since, as Richardson (1973a) observes, 'space itself and the existence of transport costs limits competition' (p. 22). Indeed, 'space' can be at the origin of market failures, leading to imperfect competition (Martin 2000).

Alternative theories of regional growth, based on the Keynesian arguments, predict regionally imbalanced (differential) growth as an inherent feature of the economic system. This problem is part of a wider concern: the process of 'cumulative-causation', a notion proposed by Myrdal (1957). Once growth has begun in the former, spatial flows of labour, capital and commodities develop spontaneously to support it. Such flows operate, however, as 'backwash effects' upon the remaining regions of the country; since faced with the higher returns obtainable in the growth regions, these other regions tend to lose not only their more skilled and enterprising workers but also much of their locally generated capital. At the same time, goods and services originating in the expanding regions flood the markets of the remaining regions, putting out of business what little secondary and tertiary industry may already have developed there. A further type of backwash effects operates through non-economic factors, such as provision of poorer health and education services in the stagnating regions as compared with the expanding regions. In all these ways, backwash effects, particularly those working through spatial interaction, come into operation to frustrate growth in the former and sustain it in the latter (Keeble 1968).

The process of cumulative-causation through the combined accelerator-multiplier effect[1] produces increasing returns in the favoured region. Financial aid may lead to centripetal forces that favour the centre to the detriment of peripheral areas instead of reducing disparities. It stands to reason, therefore, that investment begets more investment, which *perpetuates* 'inherited' regional inequalities. Due to substantial differences or 'asymmetries' in per capita income during an initial time, the lagging regions are not likely to acquiesce to more 'equitable' distribution of national income, a compelling argument for the necessity of regional policy. Clearly, in this case there is a negative relation between 'aggregate efficiency' and 'regional equity'. Richardson (1977) imposes a kind of 'inevitability' in this trade-off. Before considering this issue, however, it is important to examine briefly some cases that result in conflicts in regional policy.

3.3 Regional Policy: A Substitution Between Equity and Efficiency?

Several conflicts arise when 'space' is taken into consideration.[2] The debate can be traced back to the 1970s (e.g. Mera 1973; Ohtsuki 1971; O'Farrell 1970, 1971; Courbis 1979; Tabata 1976), if not earlier (e.g. Stevens 1958; Mera 1967; Foster and Smith 1969; Siebert 1969). As one inspects the chronology of each of the individual models,[3] one finds that they are chained together. The debate resurfaced with a vengeance in the 1980s and the 1990s (e.g. Bagchi et al. 1981; Nijkamp and Rietveld 1982; Higgins and Savoie 1995). The beginning of the present century, however, brought a rapidly growing field of research on the conflicts of regional policy, mainly with reference to the EU or individual countries (e.g. Mancha-Novarro and Garrido-Yserte 2008; Wishlade 2008; Clinch and O'Neill 2009; Bański 2010; Ezcurra and Rodríguez-Pose 2014; Silva and Leichenko 2004). The remainder of this section briefly examines particular cases that imply a conflict in the aims of regional policy.

A frequently observed phenomenon in the development process is the interregional migration of capital and labour force. It is argued that capital (labour) flows from rich (poor) to poor (rich) regions are consistent with efficiency and result in interregional equity. Population outmigration may reduce the productive ability of this region or more accurately to reduce the productivity of capital, if this factor is defined in broad sense, that is, including human capital. More educated and skilled workers may migrate when no jobs are locally available or wages are found to be insufficient (Garcia-Milà and McGuire 1992). To quote Grigg (1973) 'As the young and able migrate, so there is less labour to attract industrialists; the outflow of capital means less provision of education, health services, and transport facilities; and thus there is less to attract migrants or industry, and more incentive to emigrate' (p. 31). A policy to influence the movement of capital, however, is considerably more popular than one to induce migration. Yet it would be erroneous to assume that these two strategies are in conflict; in many cases the most rational solution to the development problems of a specific region might be a continuation of outmigration and an inflow of capital, industry and technological expertise (Richardson 1977). There is, according to Pullen (1966), 'scope for increasing the national output by employing factors, especially labour, in regions where unemployment is relatively high' (p. 108).

A policy based on the provision of incentives to firms in order to relocate in less developed regions may cause a serious conflict.[4] 'If financial incentives offered by local planners encourage new firms to locate in a lagging region, when they would have located in a more advanced region, then the underdeveloped region may be inefficiently supporting an industry in a location where it is suboptimal for that industry to conduct business' (Dawkins 2003, p. 152). In other words, the provision of relocating incentives may result in some improvements in interregional equity but incurs a significant cost in terms of overall efficiency, reflected by the 'suboptimality' in the industrial sector as a whole. O'Farrell (1974), on the other hand, argues that the provision of 'additional jobs is not in conflict to maximise economic efficiency provided that the capital used for the job creation does not yield a higher social marginal productivity at an alternative location' (p. 454).

Certain activities can be carried on most efficiently if they are clustered together than dispersed. Concentration of industry in selected points in space might increase aggregate efficiency, but it is questionable if it contributes to a reduction of interregional inequalities. An increasing interest in regional competitiveness and more concern on the positive effects of regional urban centres in promoting regional growth may cause conflict, in the sense that efficiency of the region as a whole is increased but intraregional equity is skewed. This has led Hirschman (1958) to argue that 'interregional inequality of growth is an inevitable concomitant and condition of growth itself' (p. 183).

Furthermore, it is not all clear that policies which benefit depressed regions also benefit poor people in these regions. It is quite possible that policies reducing interregional inequalities to increase inequalities within regions. As Martin (2000) notes 'the equity motive behind regional policies is thus not as straightforward as it seems because it requires a choice on reducing one type of inequality at the expense of another type of inequality' (p. 72).

A 'trade-off' arises if regional policy is considered in isolation from other policies. Evans and Martin (1991), for example, note that if aid is granted, the conclusion that the aid distorts competition is almost automatic. Indeed, if the emphasis of competition policy is exclusively focused on the efficiency and effectiveness of State aid, then this might be a potential source of conflict between regional and competition policy. Another example of conflicts can be found in the system of 'shared management, since regional policy is carried out by national and regional bodies in partnership with the European Commission. The aims of these organisations do not necessarily coincide, since EU Member-States have different traditions in terms of what constitutes regional policy. It has been suggested that complexity of regional policy does not allow the agents involved to understand its aims fully. The sphere of policy action is broad (Bachtler et al. 2003). Conflicts arise from what Polverari and Michie (2011) call 'narrow' and 'broad' policies. 'Narrow' regional policies involve strategies and interventions targeted to specific regions, while 'broad' regional policies consist of the territorial differentiation of wider policies for economic development, competitiveness and growth.

National and regional objectives are often strongly interrelated (Stilwell 1972). National economic policy always has either an explicit or implicit regional dimension, although with dubious results. In the analysis of economic development, according to Reiner (1965), 'nation and region frequently receive distinct treatment in conceptualisation as well as in administration' and 'study at the two geographical levels (nation and region) of the objectives underlying the policies and the more specific targets, as these are elements along an end-means continuum, should be most helpful in our attempt to get a deeper understanding of the interplay of values in conflict' (p. 110).

Conflicts in regional policy can be attributed, at least partly, from the different views on the 'regional' and the 'national' *scale* adopted by policy-makers, a situation evident in the 'spillover effects' from Cohesion Policy[5] over national policies, distorting regional policy effects[6]—a point raised by

Rodriguez-Pose and Fratesi (2004). It is this aspect of policy decisions that underlies the potential conflict between national and regional economic objectives (Stilwell 1972). As pointed out by Vietorisz (1967), if a national plan has been formulated independently, the inconsistencies between the set of area plans and the national plan have to be resolved.

The examples discussed so far imply a kind 'inevitability' to the trade-off in the aims of regional policy. Nevertheless, this is not always the case. Haveman (1977) argues that if investment destined for a region was induced into a depressed (or lagging) region because of some policy measure, there would be no gain or loss in national efficiency, provided that the productivity of capital were the same in both regions. This argument is hardly tenable in the sense that this case is merely theoretical. A policy which indubitably reduces regional disparities is attracting firms from other regions. If this policy, however, promotes national (aggregate) growth is questionable. It is conceivable, on the other hand, that by inducing local enterprise, it is possible to achieve both efficiency and equity (Chinitz 1966).

As it may be surmised from the above, regional policy often, but not always, is characterised by a 'trade-off'. The existing literature offers only illustrative possibilities of overcoming the trade-off in the aims of regional policy. What is missing is a general theoretical framework that could initiate and pursue the more ambitious agenda of regional policy.

3.4 Trade-Off and Regional Allocation of Investment

Non-conventional theories of regional growth theories predict regionally imbalanced growth as an inherent feature of the economic system. Spatial differences in economic performance, rather than setting off automatic self-correcting processes, are just as likely to be self-reinforcing: spatial economic imbalance, in the sense of regional disparities in growth and incomes, may not only be persistent but also in fact intensify over time (Gardiner et al. 2013).

Nevertheless, the general problem can be stated rather simply. Do policies of regional allocation of investment enhance or reverse this situation? Stewart and Streeten (1976) note the elements that determine the choice of strategy is, inter alia, the technical possibilities, the power of decision-makers and the 'initial situation'. These elements are important in determining the choice of the various development strategies, which essentially is a set of policies. In terms of the model in Chap. 2, technical possibilities are expressed by the production function,[7] while the power of decision-makers is reflected in the assumption that government allocates the 'fund'. An assumption, however, that relates to the 'initial situation' or more correctly the 'initial state' with respect to differences in regional incomes is not considered in the analysis by Intriligator (1964). It is important, therefore, to make some assumptions about the initial level of interregional inequalities. In order to have a concrete vocabulary, define the difference or the 'gap' in regional incomes as follows:

$$\Delta Y_{1,2}(t_0) \equiv Y_1(t_0) - Y_2(t_0) \equiv G_{1,2}(t_0) \tag{3.1}$$

Let $\gamma_1 - \gamma_2 > 0$ and $v_1 - v_2 > 0$, which results in $G_{1,2}(t_0) > 0$.[8] As shown in Chap. 2, the optimal allocation policy in this case is $\delta^* = 1$, $\forall t \in [t_0 \ldots T]$, which maximises $\Upsilon_N \forall t$. An increasing tendency in $G_{1,2}(t)$, however, is also evident. It may be instructive to examine this argument schematically.

In this figure time (t) is measured horizontally, and on the vertical axis Υ_N and $G_{i,2}$ are measured. As Fig. 3.1 indicates $\partial \Upsilon_N / \partial t > 0$ and $\partial G_{i,2} / \partial t > 0$ $\forall t \in [t_0 \ldots T]$, while $G_{1,2}(T) - G_{i,2}(t_0) > 0$ and $\Upsilon_N(T) - \Upsilon_N(t_0) > 0$. Given the assumption that $\gamma_1 - \gamma_2 > 0$, it is reasonable to conclude

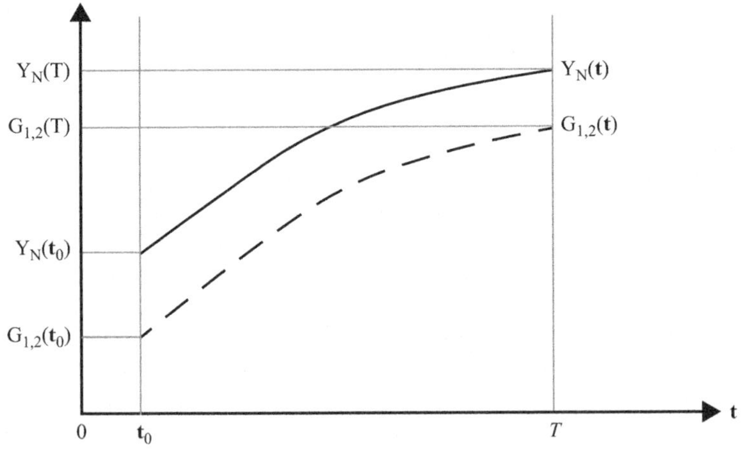

Fig. 3.1 Trade-off between efficiency and equity

that gains in aggregate efficiency are due to losses in regional equity. To be more specific, in this example the initially 'rich' region grows at the expense of the initially 'poor' region.[9] This is a clear case of 'polarised' regional growth. The reason for this resides in the fact that allocating funds in region 1 enhances the growth differentials and maintains the status quo of an initial 'core-periphery' pattern. As Fig. 3.1 shows, an upward 'spiral' is set in motion by applying the policy $\delta^* = 1 \forall t \in [t_0 \ldots T]$, which leads to $G_{i,2}(t_0) \rightarrow G_{1,2}(T)$ with $G_{i,2}(t_0) - G_{1,2}(T) < 0$. This difference approximates the cost of choosing 'too much efficiency' by policy-makers. It is quite possible that initial investment will bring more investment, which perpetuates 'inherited' regional inequalities or the structure of 'core-periphery' economy. The concentration of economic power, wealth, innovation and productivity in few regions (the 'core' of the economy) serves to maintain the core's advantage in exchange and allow core region institutions to determine the development path of the peripheral regions. Such unequal relations may be reinforced by the implementation of economic policies which favour the core at the expense of the periphery. Moreover, this situation tends to take a permanent character through mechanisms induced by migration and capital flows from 'periphery' to 'core'. Clearly, the policy $\delta^* = 1 \forall t \in [t_0 \ldots T]$ is a part of a process that leads to progressive concentration of economic activities in the core[10] and sustains an unequal spatial structure. Inequalities, according to Stewart and Streeten (1976), 'tend to beget policies which lead to accentuation of inequalities; the riches of the nouveaux riches bestow power and influence; this power and influence is then exerted to enforce policies which extend their power and wealth, and to thwart policies which threaten them' (p. 392). The same logic suggests that the policy $\delta^* = 1 \forall t \in [t_0 \ldots T]$ is, in fact, a factor that obstructs overall development even though other conditions would permit it. This strengthens the argument that such policies constitute a 'development bottleneck'. 'Concentrated' allocation policies are in accordance with the view that unequal regional development promotes aggregate growth. Such policies may be nationally efficient, but they result in persisting interregional inequalities.[11] Here lies the 'dilemma' of regional policy: growth of the economy as a whole or reduction of regional inequalities? This dilemma seems almost ineluctable. The objective function aims to maximise national income, and a concern for regional inequalities is not included.

The analysis in Chap. 2 is based on the 'truism' that in a region with an increasing value of s_i, this contributes to the increase of production efficiency. A relatively high level of s_i, however, does not necessarily imply productive investment. Unproductive investment[12] can stifle growth, and the economy is not operating efficiently. And not inconsequently, regional disparities increase. This is depicted in Fig. 3.2.

Consider, by way of illustration in Fig. 3.2, $\partial Y_N/\partial t<0$ and $\partial G_{1,2}/\partial t>0$ $\forall t\in[t_0...T]$; a situation implying significant losses in terms of aggregate efficiency, the second arm of regional policy, depicted by $Y_N(t_0)-Y_N(T)>0$. It is obviously true that the 'gap' in regional incomes increases also, as reflected by the difference $G_{i,2}(t_0)-G_{1,2}(T)<0$.

Assume that at a point in time, let t', additional investment in an initially rich region causes diseconomies or 'de-glomeration economies' that increase the attractiveness of a relatively poor region due to low labour and raw material prices, for example, a process which leads to de-concentration of investment from 'core' regions. A short way of expressing this situation is $\partial Y_N/\partial t<0\forall t\in[t_0...t'[$ and $\partial Y_N/\partial t<0$, $\forall t\in[t'...T]$, together with $\partial G_{1,2}/\partial t>0$ $\forall t\in[t_0...T]$. This can be considered to be a 'polarisation reversal', a turning point when polarisation trends give way to dispersion (Richardson 1974).

Stilwell (1972) claims that the conflict between national and regional objectives can be solved only by integrating the sectoral and regional decisions

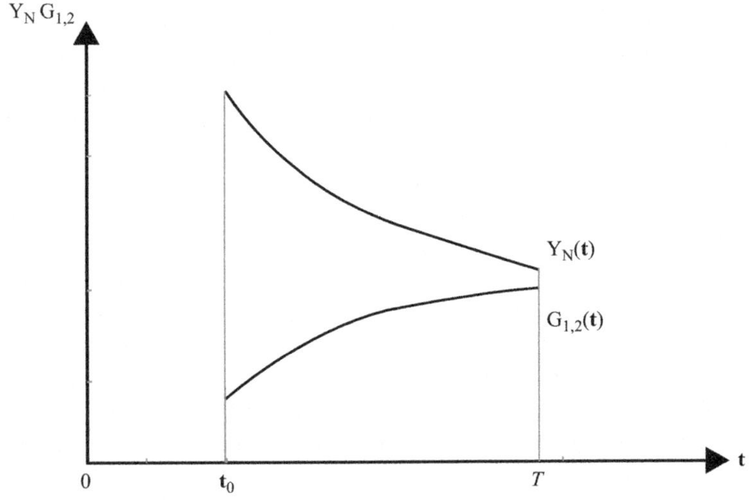

Fig. 3.2 An alternative case of trade-off between efficiency and equity

into a simultaneous decision model. It would be of interest to dwell a bit more on that possibility. All locations are not equally suited to a particular form of economic activity. Due to the uneven spatial distribution of a country's resources, the growth and decline of industry is not spread evenly, and 'there will be a kaleidoscopic pattern of differentials in income per head between regions over time' (Pullen 1966, p. 109). Consider a two-region setting and suppose that the economy in each region is divided into two sectors. Each sector provides some inputs to the other, while agents in each sector consume part of the other sector's final output. In this sense the two sectors are interdependent. Assume further that the relatively 'rich' region is specialised in technologically dynamic industries and the 'poor' region in low productivity (e.g. agriculture) or 'traditional' sectors (e.g. steel, textile), namely declining 'lag' industries[13] with rapidly shrinking markets and rising unemployment.[14] What can that possibly mean? Quite simply, this region is characterised by a relatively low value of the capital coefficient. This, combined with a relatively low propensity to save,[15] implies that this region grows at a rate considerably less than the initially rich region. Following the analysis in Chap. 2, the optimal policy is to allocate the fund in the advanced region.[16] The regional polarisation of investment inherent in the structure of the model maximises national income, but due to the interdependence of sectors (or the development of symbiotic relationships in industry[17]), agglomeration will be increased in the initially rich region causing a high degree of spatial 'imbalance', something which has become a widely accepted 'economic truth'. It is conceivable that action has to be taken to redress this 'imbalance'. Such action, according to Chisholm (1968) 'will be motivated by social and political needs and it is entirely legitimate that these should have precedence over economic considerations' (p. 172). Section 3.3 attempts to develop policies along those lines.

3.5 Regional Allocation of Investment and Regional Equity

Assume that government aims to maximise a weighted sum of regional income levels (Kendrick 1971), that is, $\text{Max}\sum_{r}\omega_r\left(p_r / p\right)\left(\overline{y}_r / p_r\right)$ with $\overline{y}_r > y_{t_0}$, where ω_r is an arbitrary weight for region r; p_r is the level of population in region r; $\overline{y}_r$ is the lower bound of income in region r, which is assumed to be exogenously determined; and p is the national population. With weights ω_r set equal to one for each region, this criterion function is for maximisation of national per capita income. By varying the weights parametrically, one can trace out a set of solutions, which correspond to a different set of relative weights for the two regions. The loss to one region would just be equal to the gain in per capita income in the other. In such cases there would be little efficiency loss from changes in the division of per capita income between the two regions. Of course, as pointed out by Kendrick (1971), 'each region may find little consolation in the knowledge that its per capita income can be transferred to the other region with small losses in the transfer' (pp. 274–275).

A possible solution to the dilemma of regional policy can be found in linear programming (e.g. Leven 1964; Reiner 1963, 1965). According to this approach, the national objective is considered as primary and the regional objective as a *constraint* on its achievement. The problem at hand is to maximise the national rate of growth, subject to the condition that income in the poorest region does not fall relative to the national average. To take a simple illustration, assume a two-region economy, denoted by *a* and *b*. Per capita incomes in each region are Y_a and Y_b, with $Y_a - Y_b > 0$. Each region grows at a rate γ_a and γ_b. The objective function in this case is $\text{Max}\, Y_p = (Y_a\gamma_a + Y_b\gamma_b)$, subject to the constraint $\gamma_b - \gamma_a \geq 0$. As a general rule, the regional objective is operative only when its effect is in opposition to the regional effects implicit in policy decisions based on national objectives. This means that there will be a conflict between regional and national objectives only when the least prosperous region has a comparative disadvantage in the sector which is the most productive from the national growth viewpoint. Then the allocation of investment would have been the same if either the national or the regional objectives had been ignored (Stilwell 1972). Balanced regional development implies that resources should be distributed geographically in an inverse proportion to the existing level of welfare (Robock 1960). This tends to produce a smaller share of expenditure for lagging regions, while a still smaller share is implied by an allocation in direct proportion to population.

Reiner (1965) argues that the allocation parameter varies according to regional multipliers (*M*). Assume that a 'fund', let X_i, has to be allocated between the two regions. The aim is to equalise per capita incomes by a predetermined (target) date. Given the level of per capita income and population in each region, denoted by Y_i and N_i respectively, the portion of the fund to be allocated to region *a* is $X_a = [(Y_b + M_b X)/N_b - Y_a/N_a]/[(M_a/N_a) + (M_b/N_b)]$, implying that the amount of fund that region *b* receives is equal to $X - X_a$. This allocation method equates per capita incomes in the two regions within a given time period.[18]

An alternative approach would be to impose $X_a = (\Upsilon_b X/N_b)/[(\Upsilon_b/N_b) + (\Upsilon_a/\Upsilon_a)]$, which tends to produce a relatively smaller share of expenditure for the less prosperous region since the multiplier effects are ignored. Obviously, this allocation method does not result in complete equalisation of per capita incomes (given that $M > 1$). A still smaller share for the less prosperous region is implied by an allocation according to direct proportion to population.[19] Such a criterion underlines several expenditure policies, particularly those related to social services whether an equalisation in prosperity depends inter alia upon the relative size of the regional multipliers. If the multiplier effect is greater in the least prosperous region, such an allocation will tend to narrow regional differences, but if it is greater in the more prosperous region, the tendency will be for regional differentials to widen (Stilwell 1972).

Another possible way to mitigate interregional disparities is by applying policies of 'partial' allocation. In this case, each region is allocated only a portion of the fund, instead of receiving the fund. If the usual assumption of positive but diminishing marginal productivity of capital is retained, then it is expected that this policy would lead to the regional *dispersion* of investment (Domazlicky 1978). The allocation parameter may also be proportional to $\Upsilon_i(t_0)$ so the highest-income region receives the minimum distribution. As the portion of the fund that the poor region gets increases, then it is reasonable to expect that $\partial G_{1,2}/\partial t < 0 \, \forall \, t \in [t_0 \ldots T]$; a 'harmonisation effect'. Most obviously, as discussed earlier, policies which successfully lead to equalisation of regional income might well have regressive effects on national growth. Choosing too much 'equity' entails sacrificing some measure of efficiency[20] (Kenworthy 1995), which is an 'inbuilt' bias in such models. Which 'strategic focus' enables to obtain maximum income for the economy as a whole and simultaneously reduce regional income inequalities?

A possible solution to the dilemma of regional policy is by attaching an appropriate weight to each region, let ω_i, and differentiating the allocation parameter accordingly[21]: $\delta = f(\omega_i)$, with $f > 0$. Government aims to maximise national income at a terminal time. The target function, therefore, can be written as $\underset{\delta}{\mathrm{Max}}\, Y'_N(T)$, where $Y'_N = \omega_1 Y_1 + \omega_2 Y_2$. The weights attached to each region are, in fact, flexible coefficients, determined by deliberate policy over time (through appropriate measures). This might very well be a fruitful angle from which to appraise the possibility of achieving the two aims simultaneously and overcome the conflict between regional equity and aggregate efficiency. Of particular importance are the assumptions that $\omega_1 - \omega_2 \neq 0$ and $\omega_i \in]0\ 1[\ \forall i = 1,2$. More technically, $\exists\ \omega_i \ni Y_N(t) = \omega_1 Y_1(t) + \omega_2 Y_2(t)\ \ \forall t \in [t_0 \ldots T]$. Let $\omega_1 = 0$, given that $\omega_1 + \omega_2 = 1$, then $Y_N = \omega_2 Y_2$. By definition, however, $Y_i \neq 0 \forall t \in [t_0 \ldots T]$ or $Y_i > 0 \forall t \in [t_0 \ldots T]$. Since $\omega_2 = 1 - \omega_1$ and assuming that $\omega_1 = 1$, then $\omega_2 = 0$; in this case $Y_N = \omega_1 Y_1$. Clearly, this is a contradiction, since by definition $Y_i \neq 0$, $\forall i = 1,2$. Consequently, $\omega_i \in]0\ 1[\ \forall i = 1,2$. To complete the set of assumptions, an initial condition with respect to per capita income in each region is necessary. In particular assume that $\Delta Y_{1,2}(t_0) > 0$, which is considered as 'unacceptable' by the government. If $\Delta Y_{1,2}$ at t_0 cannot be tolerated both socially and economically, then action has to be decided in order to eliminate it. Interpreted in this way, a necessary condition, then, would be $\omega_1 - \omega_2 < 0$, a 'bias' in favour of the economically 'anaemic' region.

The Hamiltonian function, $H = [\delta(p_1 - p_2) + p_2](\gamma_1 K_1 + \gamma_2 K_2)$, implies $p_1(t) - p_2(t) = p_2(t)(\Delta\gamma_{1,2}/\gamma_2)$. Attaching ω_i in the objective function modifies the terminal conditions as follows: $p_1(T) = \omega_1 v_1$ and $p_2(T) = \omega_2 v_2$; hence, $p_1(T) - p_2(T) = [(\omega_1 v_1 - \omega_2 v_2)/\omega_2 v_2]\, p_2(T)$.

Lemma 1 If $\gamma_1 > \gamma_2$, then $\delta^*(t) = 1$ at $0 \leq t < T$, while $\delta^*(t) = 0$ if $\gamma_1 < \gamma_2$.

Proof If $\gamma_1 > \gamma_2$, then $p_1(t) > p_2(t)$; $\therefore \delta^*(t) = 1$. Similarly, $\gamma_1 < \gamma_2$ implies $p_1(t) < p_2(t)$; $\therefore \delta^*(t) = 0$. Q.E.D.

Lemma 2 If $\omega_1 v_1 > \omega_2 v_2$, $\delta^*(t) = 1$ at $t = T$, while $\delta^*(t) = 0$ if $\omega_1 v_1 < \omega_2 v_2$.

Proof If $\omega_1 v_1 > \omega_2 v_2$, then $p_1(T) - p_2(T) > 0$; $\therefore \delta^*(t) = 1$ at $t = T$. Similarly, $\omega_1 v_1 < \omega_2 v_2$ implies $\delta^*(t) = 0$. Q.E.D.

The investment sequence when $\omega_1 > \omega_2$ is set out in Table 3.1, while Table 3.2 gives the optimal allocation of investment when government imposes $\omega_1 < \omega_2$.

What does that mean for regional policy standpoint? Propositions 1 and 2 attempt to answer this question.

Table 3.1 Allocation matrix: $\omega_1 > \omega_2$

	$\gamma_1 > \gamma_2$		$\gamma_1 < \gamma_2$	
	$v_1 > v_2$	$v_1 < v_2$	$v_1 > v_2$	$v_1 < v_2$
$\gamma_1 - \gamma_2$	$\gamma_1 - \gamma_2 > 0$	$\gamma_1 - \gamma_2 > 0$	$\gamma_1 - \gamma_2 < 0$	$\gamma_1 - \gamma_2 < 0$
$p_1(T) - p_2(T)$	$\omega_1 v_1 - \omega_2 v_2 > 0$	$\omega_1 v_1 - \omega_2 v_2 > 0$	$\omega_1 v_1 - \omega_2 v_2 > 0$	$\omega_1 v_1 - \omega_2 v_2 > 0$
$\delta^*(t)$ at $0 \leq t < T$	1	1	0	0
$\delta^*(t)$ at $t = T$	1	1	1	1

Table 3.2 Allocation matrix: $\omega_1 < \omega_2$

	$\gamma_1 > \gamma_2$		$\gamma_1 < \gamma_2$	
	$v_1 > v_2$	$v_1 < v_2$	$v_1 > v_2$	$v_1 < v_2$
$\gamma_1 - \gamma_2$	$\gamma_1 - \gamma_2 > 0$	$\gamma_1 - \gamma_2 > 0$	$\gamma_1 - \gamma_2 < 0$	$\gamma_1 - \gamma_2 < 0$
$p_1(T) - p_2(T)$	$\omega_1 v_1 - \omega_2 v_2 < 0$	$\omega_1 v_1 - \omega_2 v_2 < 0$	$\omega_1 v_1 - \omega_2 v_2 < 0$	$\omega_1 v_1 - \omega_2 v_2 < 0$
$\delta^*(t)$ at $0 \leq t < T$	1	1	0	0
$\delta^*(t)$ at $t = T$	0	0	0	0

Proposition 1 If $\gamma_1 > \gamma \wedge G_{1,2}(t_0) > 0$, then $\delta^*(t) = 1$ at $0 \leq t < T \wedge \delta^*(t) = 0$ at $t = T$.

Proof If $\gamma_1 > \gamma_2$, according to Lemma 1 $\delta^*(t) = 1$ at $0 \leq t < T$. If $\omega_1 < \omega_2$, Lemma 2 implies $p_1(T) - p_2(T) < 0$; $\therefore \delta^*(t) = 0$ at $t = T$. Q.E.D.

Proposition 2 If $\gamma_1 < \gamma_2$, $G_{1,2}(t_0) > 0 \wedge \omega_1 < \omega$ then $\delta^*(t) = 0$, $\forall t \in [0 \ldots T]$.

Proof According to Lemma 1 at $0 \leq t < T$ $\delta^*(t) = 0$ if $\gamma_1 > \gamma_2$; $\omega_1 < \omega_2$ in tandem with Lemma 2 implies $\delta^*(t) = 0$ at $t = T$, $\therefore \delta^*(t) = 0 \forall t \in [0 \ldots T]$. Q.E.D.

Obviously, Proposition 1 implies income maximisation at $0 \leq t < T$, since $Y_N(T) - Y_N(t_0) > 0$. A subsequent switch in δ alleviates regional inequalities, since $\omega_1 < \omega_2$ reverses the difference $v_1 > v_2$ in favour of region 2 (provided of course that $\omega_2 \to 1$). Similarly, $\delta^*(t) = 1$ at $0 \leq t < T$ and $\delta^*(t) = 0$ at $t = T$ offers an opportunity to overcome the 'trade-off' if $v_1 < v_2$.

Assume that $\gamma_1 < \gamma_2$; the optimal policy is then $\delta^*(t) = 0 \forall t \in [0 \ldots T]$. Apparently, the condition $\gamma_1 < \gamma_2$, in conjunction with the initial assumption that $G_{1,2}(t_0) > 0$, implies maximisation of total output and at the same time contributes to a significant reduction of regional disparities. According to Proposition 2, at $t = T$ the fund is invested in region 2 irrespective of the difference in the capital coefficients. It is important to note, however, that such conclusions are valid as long as the condition $\omega_1 < \omega_2$ is imposed by policy-makers, a necessary prerequisite in order to change the optimality conditions in favour of the relatively poor region. As implied by the structure of the model, this condition results in $\omega_1 v_1 - \omega_2 v_2 < 0$. In other words, the weight attached to region 2 should be sufficiently large in order to reverse the difference $v_1 - v_2 > 0$.

Following a procedure similar to that in Sect. 2.5, the switching time when a weight is attached to each region can be estimated as follows:

$$t^{\omega} = T - (1/\gamma_2)\log\left\{\left[(\omega_2 s_1 - \omega_1 s_2)v_1\right]/\left[(\gamma_1 - \gamma_2)\omega_2\right]\right\} \quad (3.2)$$

Tables 3.3 and 3.4 compare the switching time proposed in Chap. 2 with that implied by Eq. (3.9), when $\omega_1 > \omega_2$ and $\omega_1 < \omega_2$, respectively.

It is clear from Tables 3.3 and 3.4 that the switching time is affected not only from changes in the parameters of the model, but also it depends critically on the value of ω_i. Imposing different values to the weights, therefore, enables a regular change of the switching time according to the priorities of regional policy set by policy-makers. Rather what is needed is a change in the weights, as economic development proceeds.

In bringing this section to a close, it is important to note that the allocation policies implied by Propositions 1 and 2 should be considered in

Table 3.3 Switching times when $\omega_1 > \omega_2$

$t^* > t^{\omega}$	$v_1 > v_2$, $s_1 < s_2$, $\gamma_1 < \gamma_2$
$t^* < t^{\omega}$	$v_1 < v_2$, $s_1 > s_2$, $\gamma_1 > \gamma_2$
$t^* > t^{\omega}$	$v_1 < v_2$, $s_1 < s_2$, $\gamma_1 < \gamma_2$

Table 3.4 Switching times when $\omega_1 < \omega_2$

$t^* < t^\omega$	$v_1 > v_2$, $s_1 < s_2$, $\gamma_1 < \gamma_2$
$t^* > t^\omega$	$v_1 < v_2$, $s_1 > s_2$, $\gamma_1 > \gamma_2$
$t^* < t^\omega$	$v_1 < v_2$, $s_1 < s_2$, $\gamma_1 < \gamma_2$

conjunction with the conditions $G_{1,2}(t_0) > 0$ and $G_{1,2}(t_0) < 0$. In the first case, government sets $\omega_1 < \omega_2$, while in the second case, $\omega_1 > \omega_2$ seems to be more appropriate. But ambiguity remains. The two aims are still treated as diametrically different. Consequently, it is not very useful to dwell further on speculations about the probabilities of compatibly in aims unless a concern for interregional inequalities is introduced *explicitly*. An appropriate framework is by employing a 'dual' objective function, as will be seen in Sect. 3.4.

3.6 Introducing 'Equity' in the Objective Function

The purpose of this section is in part expository, in part critical. How important is inequality across regions? Persistent regional inequalities are nationally inefficient since the underutilisation of productive capacity in the 'lagging' regions indicates that prosperity of the economy as a whole is lower than it could otherwise be (Martin 2008). Spatially unbalanced development and growth may bias or even compromise national economic policy. Such social equity and national efficiency arguments would thus appear to provide a strong rationale for regional policies aimed at reducing the degree and scale of geographical imbalance in the economy (Gardiner et al. 2013). These arguments clearly indicate the need for introducing the aim of regional equity explicitly in the objective function. In this respect, the analysis by Michel et al. (1983) is of particular importance. More specifically, the objective function employed takes the following form:

$$\dot{Y} = Y_N / L_N - G_{1,2}^2 \tag{3.3}$$

In Eq. (3.3) $L_N = L_1 + L_2$ is total labour force and $G_{1,2} = (Y/L)_1 - (Y/L)_2$. This function treats the two aims as independent and, therefore, is expressed in an additive form.[22] In other words, this objective function attempts to portray a 'redistribution without destroying wealth' problem.

One way of solving multi-dimensional optimisation problems is by weighting the individual variables. To that effect, a weight, let ω, is attached to the aim of regional equity. Given the relationship that characterises production,[23] the objective function appears as follows:

$$\underset{\delta_1,\delta_2}{\text{Max}}\left\{a_1K_1(T)+a_2K_2(T)-\omega\left[c_1K_1(T)-c_2K_2(T)\right]^2\right\} \tag{3.4}$$

where $a_i = v_i/L_N$ and $c_i = v_i/L_i$.

It should be noted that the weight attached to regional equity should be positive and sufficiently large, so that the aim of aggregate efficiency is not dominated by the aim of regional equity. It is assumed that a proportion of savings of region 1 (2) is transferred to region 2 (1): $\delta_i \in [0,1]$, $i=1,2$. This process gives rise to 'losses' or 'transfer cost' (ε_i) depending on interregional income differences. Richardson (1974) claims that investment is less costly if the fund is invested in the region that has the savings. Assuming that $S_i = f(Y_i)$, then ε_i can be treated as a direct proportion to the existing levels of income. Alternatively, ε_i can be defined as a constant percentage of savings from region j to region i: $\varepsilon_i \in [0,1], \forall j \neq i$. Consequently,

$$\dot{K}_1 = (1-\delta_1)\gamma_1K_1 + (1-\varepsilon_1)\delta_2\gamma_2K_2 \tag{3.5}$$

$$\dot{K}_2 = (1-\delta_2)\gamma_2K_2 + (1-\varepsilon_2)\delta_1\gamma_1K_1 \tag{3.6}$$

The Hamiltonian associated to this problem is

$$H = \delta_1\gamma_1K_1\left[p_2(1-\varepsilon_2)-p_1\right] + \delta_2\gamma_2K_2\left[p_1(1-\varepsilon_1)-p_2\right] + p_1\gamma_1K_1 + p_2\gamma_2K_2 \tag{3.7}$$

The ad-joint equations are defined as follows:

$$\dot{p}_1 = -\partial H / \partial K_1 = -\gamma_1 \max\left[p_1,(1-\varepsilon_2)p_2\right] = -\gamma_1\left[p_1(1-\delta_1)+p_2(1-\varepsilon_2)\delta_1\right] \tag{3.8}$$

$$\dot{p}_2 = -\partial H / \partial K_2 = -\gamma_2 \max\left[p_2,(1-\varepsilon_1)p_1\right] = -\gamma_2\left[p_1(1-\varepsilon_1)\delta_2 + p_2(1-\delta_2)\right] \tag{3.9}$$

The terminal conditions, $P_i(T) = \partial\dot{Y}(T) / \partial K_i(T)$, imply

$$P_1(T) = a_1 - 2\omega c_1\left[c_1K_1(T) - c_2K_2(T)\right] \text{or } P_1(T) = a_1 - 2\omega c_1 G_{1,2} \quad (3.10)$$

$$P_2(T) = a_2 - 2\omega c_2\left[c_2K_2(T) - c_1K_1(T)\right] \text{or } P_2(T) = a_2 + 2\omega c_2 G_{1,2} \quad (3.11)$$

Setting $\partial H/\partial_i = 0, \gamma_1 K_1[-p_1 + (1-\varepsilon_2)p_2] = 0$ and $\gamma_2 K_2[-p_2 + (1-\varepsilon_1)p_1] = 0$, hence $p_1(t) = (1-\varepsilon_2)p_2(t)$ and $p_2(t) = (1-\varepsilon_1)p_1(t)$. It follows, then, that the ratio γ_1/γ_2, which specifies the allocation policy at $[0\ldots T[$, depends upon ε_i. Essentially, Michel et al. (1983) propose a policy of partial allocation. At the beginning of the planning period, the allocation policies contribute to the aim of efficiency, while equity takes place at the end of the planning period. The linearity of Eq. (3.3) on δ_i implies that the optimal allocation policy is a sequence of phases (scenarios) depending on the relation between the auxiliary variables, that is, $[p_2(1-\varepsilon_2) - p_1]$ and $[p_1(1-\varepsilon_1) - p_2]$. At phase A, $p_2(t) < (1-\varepsilon_1)p_1(t)$, then $\delta_1(t) = 0$ and $\delta_2(t) = 1$, that is, region 1 receives the entire fund. Region 1 retains its savings and receives a portion of region 2's savings, in phase B, $\delta_1(t) = 0$ and $\delta_2(t) \in [0, 1]$, since $p_2(t) = (1-\varepsilon_1)p_1(t)$. Given that $\varepsilon_i > 0$,[24] at phase C, each region retains its own internally generated savings; $p_1(t) > (1-\varepsilon_2)p_2(t)$ and $p_2(t) > (1-\varepsilon_1)p_1(t)$, implying $\delta_i(t) = 0$; $\dot{K}_i = \gamma_i K_i$. At phase D, $p_1(t) = (1-\varepsilon_2)p_2(t)$, that is, $\delta_1(t) \in [0, 1]$ and $\delta_2(t) = 1$, that is, region 2 retains its savings and receives a part of region 1's savings. At phase E, region 2 receives the entire fund, since $p_1(t) < (1-\varepsilon_2)p_2(t)$ implies $\delta_1(t) = 1$ and $\delta_2(t) = 0$. Total savings initially are transferred to the region where capital productivity is higher in accordance with the aim of efficiency. Finally, the fund is allocated to the low-productivity region in accordance with the 'equity' criterion. Between these two periods, the two regions grow autonomously—a phase of 'autarkic growth' or 'autonomous development'. The switch in the allocation parameter occurs after this phase. If $a_1 > a_2$ (or $\gamma_1 - \gamma_2 > 0$), then the optimal policy is one of the following six scenarios: (i) phase A on $[0\ T]$, (ii) phase A on $[0\ t_0[$ and phase C on $[t_0\ T]$, (iii) phase A on $[0\ t_0[$, phase C on $[t_0\ t_1[$ and phase E on the segment $[t_1\ T]$, (iv) phase C on $[0\ T]$, (v) phase C on $[0\ t_1[$ and phase E on $[t_1\ T]$, (vi) phase E on $[0\ T]$. Michel et al. (1983) prove that the optimal policy is scenario (iii). This is entirely logical, given the structure of their model and the fact that regional equity is defined as $G_{1,2}(T) = 0$.

In the long run, all phases take place, depending on the importance that government attaches to the aim of 'regional equity'. If a relatively high weight is attached to the aim of equity, then the optimal policy is to allocate the fund to the region with the highest rate of growth and subsequently to the other region. If $\gamma_1/\gamma_2 > 1$, then the optimal policy is to invest initially in region 1, then the two regions grow autonomously, and finally the fund is allocated to region 2. This policy[25] implies that at the beginning of the planning period, efficiency dominates (continued localisation of economic development), while at the end of the planning period, equity (dispersion of economic development) takes over.[26] If per capita income in region 2 is relatively higher at the beginning of the planning period, then allocating the fund in region 1 is optimal not only from efficiency but also from equity point of view. One interesting conclusion of this approach is that government may choose to channel the fund in the most productive region for most of the time period and at the end of the period to channel it in the least productive region for equity reasons. This is a government (income redistribution) policy which can be regarded as complementary, in the sense that promotes both 'aggregate efficiency' and 'regional equity'. This is the only case of compatibility in aims.

This section began by posing an intriguing question about the significance of regional inequality in relation with national efficiency. As argued in Chap. 1, there is yet no clear or definitive answer to this question. Michel et al. (1983) showed that it is possible to incorporate effectively 'aggregate efficiency' and 'regional equity' in a 'trade-off' function. In closing this section, it is important to note that Michel et al. (1983) present the analysis in a strict mathematical way, which makes it difficult for non-mathematics to follow its logic. Indeed, according to George (1988), 'it has been suggested that mathematical analysis provides an effective 'barrier to entry' to the discipline of economics' (p. 4). Chapter 4 attempts to examine the hypothesis of compatibility in the aims of regional policy in a mathematically structured model and at the same time easily 'accessible' for readers without mathematical background.

3.7 Conclusion

Inequality, according to Robinson (1962), makes the system not only inequitable but also inefficient. This view accepts the argument that 'regional equity' and 'aggregate efficiency' are compatible rather that competitive. Only innovative governance solutions will be capable of promoting simultaneously aggregate growth and improvements of interregional equity. The economy of the future is generated, at least partly, from current decisions on investment projects. While policies that turning projects into actual investment may improve interregional equity, it is also possible to restrict growth in the economy as a whole. On the other hand, policies aiming exclusively on national growth may cause a less favourable income distribution. This case, however, can be avoided by an appropriate choice of allocation policies.

The work by Michel et al. (1983) reviewed briefly in Sect. 3.4 offers some important insights. Using a 'trade-off function' and defining 'regional equity' as absolute interregional equality, Michel et al. (1983) establish mathematically a model of optimal allocation, which essentially is a sequence of phases with partial allocation policies in each phase. A feature of particular importance is the weight attached to the aim of regional equity. If a relatively high weight is attached to the aim of equity, then the optimal policy is to allocate the fund to the region with the highest rate of growth and subsequently to the other region. Between these two phases, the two regions grow autonomously, a 'transitional' phase, since subsequently it leads to the elimination of regional inequalities. Some authors (e.g. Domazlicky 1978) argue that a 'transitional' phase is likely to be more acceptable by society. Not everyone will be convinced by this argument, however, since it is almost probable that a prolonged phase of 'autonomous development' may sustain initial interregional inequalities leading to underutilisation of resources in the long run. It stands to reason, therefore, to argue that the phase of 'autonomous' development may set up a 'cumulative' mechanism in motion, which perpetuates already established regional inequalities. The model of regional allocation of investment, therefore, has to be modified in such a way in order to avoid the phase of 'autonomous' development, implied in the approach by Michel et al. (1983). More importantly, perhaps, is a conceptual problem with the definition of regional equity as absolute interregional equality. Clearly, this is an unrealistic aim. Indeed, as Chinitz (1966) puts it, 'we certainly cannot hope to generate growth on every corner and in every hamlet' (p. 9). Setting, however, quantified aims that are both ambitious and realistic under a given performance framework, several cases of compatibility between 'regional equity' and 'aggregate efficiency' may arise. Such aims will be developed and discussed in the next chapter.

Notes

1. Pullen (1966) eloquently describes this cumulative process as 'an accelerator and subsequent multiplier effect will result from the rise in income of the rich region and the fall in the income of the poor region. The interaction of multiplier and accelerator will tend to make the change in the level of regional income a cumulative process' (p. 110).
2. As Richardson (1973b) notes, 'the trade-off thesis is attractive with its emphasis on a household's rational calculations of a choice between more space and/or cheaper housing on the one hand, and shorter journeys to work and greater accessibility on the other' (p. 22).
3. This section makes no claim to being a complete survey of the relevant literature—the purpose is only to illustrate certain major trends.
4. Taxation and subsidies inducing firms to relocate in poor regions may reduce the overall efficiency of the economy (Martin 2000). Similarly, restrictions in the movements of industry, although of negligible budgetary cost, may hide significant real costs in terms of sacrifices in national efficiency (O' Farrell 1974).
5. Initially, an adjunct to national regional policies, now a core source of expenditure for development and a cornerstone of the EU's core policies since the mid-1980s.
6. Empirical studies (e.g. Fagerberg and Verspagen 1996) suggest that regional policy often has negative impacts on regional growth.
7. Recall that the analysis attempts to develop short-run policies.
8. Assuming $G_{1,2}(t_0)=0$ will not alter the main conclusions.
9. Hirschman (1958) argues that differential regional rates in development reflect the tendency of growth to be polarised.
10. This according to Rodriguez-Pose and Fratesi (2004) is a reason that lacks the capacity of Structural Funds to promote cohesion across the regions of the EU.
11. The policy focus on what make firms more competitive (e.g. 'innovation-oriented regional policies') is based on this argument. Porter (1990), for example, argues that geographical clustering can be seen as an organising force for national competitiveness. Such policies also result in agglomeration in selected points in space (or regions). Agglomeration has 'countervailing effects: often positive in terms of efficiency, but potentially negative with regard to equity' (Martin 1999, p. 12). A similar argument can be made for clusters (Martin 1998).
12. A characteristic of unproductive investment is zero marginal productivity. This kind of investment in development economics is described as 'cathedrals in the desert', which is equivalent to the 'demonstration effect' or the 'conspicuous consumption', proposed by Veblen (1899). This is a distinct

possibility in several projects financed by the Structural Funds. There are 'substitution effects' diverting resources from more productive projects to those financed by Structural Funds, which might be unproductive.

13. Such industries do not experience autonomous expansion but depend on the expansion of 'lead' industrial sectors, located in other regions. 'Lead' industries have a higher (above the average) rate of productivity growth. Usually 'lead' industries are associated with growth-inducing impacts (lead effects) on other industries through their demand for inputs.
14. This situation characterises several less developed and developing countries. It is generally argued that the predominance of agriculture is an obstacle to growth. Although this is not necessarily true, it is important to note that regional growth is a highly related process, the components of which are inextricably linked—a development continuum (Hodder 1973) and no sector should be overemphasised as a panacea for development.
15. Rural and low-income workers, however, can have high savings rates (Hoff and Stiglitz 2001). In regions where subsistence farming is the main occupation, improvements in agriculture may permit an increase in the fraction of income saved. It is possible for the lagging region to experience a relatively rapid rate of output growth and simultaneously to generate and increasing amount of unemployment (or underemployment). Rapid growth of total output is often accompanied by a more unequal income distribution within a region. A similar argument can be made for developing countries. See Ecaus (1967).
16. A policy-maker with efficiency in mind might look at Fig. 3.1.
17. This refers to the 'con-industrialisation', a term proposed by Renner (1947).
18. This holds under certain assumptions about the offsetting nature of spillover effects between the region and constancy of multiplier value as between different sectors of expenditure injection.
19. The differentiation in the allocation parameter may also be a function of the size, the geographical area that a region covers or the density of settlements. It can be applied to investment projects for railway, irrigation and so on—elements of particular importance for regional development.
20. The foregone national income is the cost of policies aiming exclusively on 'equity', the so-called leaky bucket effect.
21. This can be seen as an attempt to 'discriminate' between different packages of regional aid support, which represents, at least partly, an interest to a specific geographical area due to political reasons.
22. Eliminating regional disparities is equivalent to minimise the objective function. A negative sign is, therefore, attached to $G_{1,2}(t)$. For more details, see Sydsæter et al. (2005).
23. See Chap. 2, Sect. 2.3.

24. If $\varepsilon_i \rightarrow 1$, then $p_i \rightarrow 0$; hence, phase C is the optimal solution.
25. This logic characterised regional policies in Japan. Until 1976, for example, egalitarian policies were applied and subsequently policies oriented towards efficiency (Mera 1986). Allocation policies of public capital after the Second World War were able to increase national product and simultaneously equalise per capita regional incomes (Merriman 1990). Yamano and Ohkawara (2000), however, claim that this policy is concentrated more on regional equity rather than aggregate efficiency.
26. In the early stages of development, efficiency is the main concern and later priority is given to equity. This is the 'inverted U' hypothesis: '[…] a statistic describing regional inequality will trace out an inverted "U" over the national growth path' (Williamson 1965, pp. 9–10). This view shares several similarities with the development theories of the 1950s and early 1960s (e.g. Rostow 1960), which viewed the process of development as a series of successive stages of economic growth through which all countries must pass.

References

Bachtler, J., Wishlade, F., & Yuill, D. (2003). *Regional Policies After 2006: Complementary or Conflict?* (European Policy Research Paper Number 51). European Policies Research Centre, University of Strathclyde.

Bagchi, A., Olsder, G., & Strijbos, R. (1981). Regional Allocation of Investment as a Hierarchical Optimization Problem. *Regional Science and Urban Economics, 11*(1), 205–213.

Bański, J. (2010). Dilemmas for Regional Development in the Concepts Seeking to Develop Poland's Spatial Structure. *Regional Studies, 44*(5), 535–549.

Borts, G., & Stein, J. (1964). *Economic Growth in a Free Market.* New York: Columbia University Press.

Chinitz, B. (1966). Appropriate Goals for Regional Economic Policy. *Urban Studies, 3*(1), 1–7.

Chisholm, M. (1968). *Rural Settlement and Land Use.* London: Hutchinson University.

Clinch, J., & O'Neill, E. (2009). Applying Spatial Economics to National Spatial Planning. *Regional Studies, 43*(2), 157–178.

Courbis, R. (1979). The REGINA Model: A Regional-National Model for French Planning. *Regional Science and Urban Economics, 9*(2–3), 117–139.

Dawkins, C. (2003). Regional Development Theory: Conceptual Foundations, Classic Works, and Recent Developments. *Journal of Planning Literature, 18*(2), 131–172.

Domazlicky, B. (1978). The Regional Allocation of Investment: A Neoclassical Model. *Journal of Regional Analysis and Policy, 8*(2), 1–13.

Ecaus, R. (1967). Planning in India. In M. Millikan (Ed.), *National Economic Planning* (pp. 305–378). Cambridge, MA: National Bureau of Economic Research.

Evans, A., & Martin, S. (1991). Socially Acceptable Distortions of Competition: Community Policy on State Aid. *European Law Review, 2*, 79–111.

Ezcurra, R., & Rodríguez-Pose, A. (2014). Trade Openness and Spatial Inequality in Emerging Countries. *Spatial Economic Analysis, 9*(2), 162–182.

Fagerberg, J., & Verspagen, B. (1996). Heading for Divergence? Regional Growth in Europe Reconsidered. *Journal of Common Market Studies, 34*(3), 431–448.

Foster, C., & Smith, J. (1969). Allocation of Central Government Budgets Over City Regions. *Urban Studies, 6*, 210–226.

Garcia-Milà, T., & McGuire, T. (1992). The Contribution of Publicly Provided Inputs to States' Economies. *Regional Science and Urban Economics, 22*(2), 229–241.

Gardiner, B., Martin, R., Sunley, P., & Tayler, P. (2013). Spatially Unbalanced Growth in the British Economy. *Journal of Economic Geography, 13*(6), 889–928.

George, D. (1988). *Mathematical Modelling for Economists*. London: Macmillan.

Grigg, D. (1973). Geographical Studies of Economic Development with Special Reference to Agriculture. In M. Chisholm & B. Rodgers (Eds.), *Studies in Human Geography* (pp. 18–84). London: Heinemann.

Haveman, R. (1977). On Evaluating the Regional Impact of Public Policy. In E. Smith (Ed.), *Explorations in Economic Research: New Directions in Federal Economic Development Programs, 4*(3), 429–444, National Bureau of Economic Research.

Higgins, B., & Savoie, D. (1995). *Regional Development Theories and Their Applications*. New Brunswick: Transaction Publishers.

Hirschman, A. (1958). *The Strategy of Economic Development*. New Haven: Yale University Press.

Hodder, B. (1973). *Economic Development in the Tropics* (2nd ed.). London: Methuen.

Hoff, K., & Stiglitz, J. (2001). Modern Economic Theory and Development. In G. Meier & J. Stiglitz (Eds.), *Frontiers of Development Economics*. Oxford: Oxford University Press.

Intriligator, M. (1964). Regional Allocation of Investment: Comment. *Quarterly Journal of Economics, 78*(4), 659–662.

Keeble, D. (1968). Models of Economic Development. In R. Chorley & P. Haggett (Eds.), *Socio-economic Models in Geography* (pp. 243–302). London: Methuen & Co.

Kendrick, D. (1971). Mathematical Models for Regional Planning. *Regional and Urban Economics, 1*(3), 247–287.

Kenworthy, L. (1995). Equality and Efficiency: The Illusory Trade-Off. *European Journal of Political Research, 27*, 225–254.

Leven, C. (1964). Establishing Goals for Regional Economic Development. *Journal of American Institute of Planners, 30*(2), 100–110.
Mancha-Novarro, T., & Garrido-Yserte, R. (2008). Regional Policy in the European Union: The Cohesion-Competitiveness Dilemma. *Regional Science Policy and Practice, 1*(1), 47–66.
Martin, P. (1998). Can Regional Policies Affect Growth and Geography in Europe? *World Economy, 21*(7), 757–774.
Martin, P. (1999). Are European Regional Policies Delivering? *European Investment Bank Papers, 4*(2), 10–23.
Martin, P. (2000). The Role of Public Policy in the Process of Regional Convergence. *European Investment Bank Papers, 5*(2), 69–79.
Martin, R. (2008). National Growth Versus Regional Equality? A Cautionary Note on the New Trade-Off Thinking in Regional Policy Discourse. *Regional Science Policy and Practice, 1*(1), 3–13.
Mera, K. (1967). Trade-Off Between Aggregate Efficiency and Interregional Equity: A Static Analysis. *Quarterly Journal of Economics, 8*, 658–674.
Mera, K. (1973). On the Urban Agglomeration and Efficiency. *Economic Development and Cultural Change, 21*, 309–324.
Mera, K. (1986). Population Stabilisation and National Spatial Policy of Public Investment: The Japanese Experience. *International Regional Science Review, 10*, 47–65.
Merriman, D. (1990). Public Capital and Regional Output: Another Look at Some Japanese and American Data. *Regional Science and Urban Economics, 20*(4), 437–458.
Michel, P., Pestieau, P., & Thisse, J. (1983). Regional Allocation of Investment with Distributive Objectives. *Journal of Regional Science, 23*(2), 199–209.
Myrdal, G. (1957). *Economic Theory and Underdeveloped Regions*. London: Duckworth.
Nijkamp, P., & Rietveld, P. (1982). Multiple Objectives in Multilevel Multiregional Planning Models. In M. Albegov, A. Andersson, & F. Snickars (Eds.), *Regional Development Modeling: Theory and Practice* (pp. 145–168). Amsterdam: North-Holland Publishing Company.
O'Farrell, P. (1970). Regional Development in Ireland: Problems of Goal Formulation and Objective Specification. *Economic and Social Review, 2*(1), 71–92.
O'Farrell, P. (1971). The Regional Problem in Ireland: Some Reflections Upon Development Strategy. *Economic and Social Review, 2*(4), 453–480.
O'Farrell, P. (1974). Regional Planning in Ireland—The Case for Concentration: A Reappraisal. *Economic and Social Review, 5*(4), 499–514.
Ohtsuki, Y. (1971). Regional Allocation of Public Investment in an n-Region Economy. *Journal of Regional Science, 11*(2), 225–233.

Osberg, L. (1995). The Equity/Efficiency Trade-Off in Retrospect. *Canadian Business Economics, 3*(3), 5–20.
Polverari, L., & Michie, R. (2011). *Complementarity or Conflict? The (In)coherence of Cohesion Policy* (European Policy Research Paper No. 78). University of Strathclyde.
Porter, M. (1990). *The Competitive Advantage of Nations.* New York: Free Press.
Pullen, M. (1966). Regional Development in the United Kingdom. In W. Birmingham & A. Ford (Eds.), *Planning and Growth in Rich and Poor Countries* (pp. 107–141). London: George Allen and Unwin.
Reiner, T. (1963). Organising Regional Investment Criteria. *Papers in Regional Science, 1*, 63–72.
Reiner, T. (1965). Sub-national and National Planning: Decision Criteria. *Papers in Regional Science, 14*, 107–136.
Renner, G. (1947). Geography of Industrial Localization. *Economic Geography, 23*(3), 167–189.
Richardson, H. (1973a). *Elements of Regional Economics.* London: Penguin.
Richardson, H. (1973b). *Urban Economics.* London: Penguin.
Richardson, H. (1974). *Regional Growth Theory.* London: Macmillan.
Richardson, H. (1977). Aggregate Efficiency and Interregional Equity. In H. Folmer & J. Oosterhaven (Eds.), *Spatial Inequalities and Regional Development* (pp. 161–183). North Holland: Martinus Nijhoff.
Robinson, J. (1962). *Economic Philosophy.* London: Penguin.
Robock, S. (1960). Regional and National Economic Development in India. *Papers in Regional Science, 6*, 65–81.
Rodríguez-Pose, A., & Fratesi, U. (2004). Between Development and Social Policies: The Impact of European Structural Funds in Objective 1 Regions. *Regional Studies, 38*(1), 97–113.
Rostow, W. (1960). *The Stages of Economic Growth: A Non–communist Manifesto.* Cambridge: Cambridge University Press.
Siebert, H. (1969). Goal Conflicts in Regional Growth Policy. *Zeitschrift für Nationalökonomie, 29*(1–2), 19–28.
Silva, J., & Leichenko, R. (2004). Regional Income Inequality and International Trade. *Economic Geography, 80*(3), 261–286.
Stevens, B. (1958). An Interregional Linear Programming Model. *Journal of Regional Science, 1*(1), 60–98.
Stewart, F., & Streeten, P. (1976). New Strategies for Development: Poverty, Income Distribution, and Growth. *Oxford Economic Papers, 28*(3), 381–405.
Stilwell, F. (1972). *Regional Economic Policy.* London: Macmillan.
Sydsæter, K., Strøm, A., & Berck, P. (2005). *Economists' Mathematical Manual.* Berlin: Springer.
Tabata, Y. (1976). Regional Economic Models and Continuous Programming. *Regional Science and Urban Economics, 6*(2), 193–204.

Veblen, T. (1899). *The Theory of the Leisure Class: An Economic Study of Institutions.* New York: B.W. Huebsch.

Vietorisz, T. (1967). Locational Choices in Planning. In M. Millikan (Ed.), *Economic Planning* (pp. 39–130). Cambridge, MA: National Bureau of Economic Research.

Williamson, J. (1965). Regional Inequality and the Process of National Development: A Description of the Patterns. *Economic Development and Cultural Change, 13*(4), 1–84.

Wishlade, F. (2008). Competition and Cohesion—Coherence or Conflict? European Union Regional State Aid Reform Post-2006. *Regional Studies, 42*(5), 753–765.

Yamano, N., & Ohkawara, T. (2000). The Regional Allocation of Public Investment: Efficiency or Equity? *Journal of Regional Science, 40*(2), 205–229.

CHAPTER 4

Compatibility Between Equity and Efficiency

Abstract Regional policies are mainly development policies and often imply a trade-off between 'regional equity' and 'aggregate efficiency'. A policy improving regional equity may incur losses in the efficiency of the economy as a whole and vice versa. This, however, is a simplistic interpretation. There is a possibility for these aims being complementary rather than competitive. This chapter develops a conceptual framework in order to detect cases of conflict-resolution, namely, cases in which the aims of 'regional equity' and 'aggregate efficiency' are compatible.

Keywords Overcoming trade-offs • Development strategy • Regional planning • Regional policy evaluation

JEL Classification R10

4.1 Introduction

A national economy is not a homogenous political or economic entity or just a set of 'spatial' divisions. It is a complex system in which several activities interact and generate *conflicts* and *complementarities*. The trade-off between 'regional equity' and 'aggregate efficiency' has shaped (and continues to do so) economic policies (Gardiner et al. 2013). The economist,

S. Alexiadis, *The Dilemma of Regional Policy*,
https://doi.org/10.1007/978-3-319-68900-5_4

however, has not only to point out the existence of the 'trade-off' but also to detect cases of compatibility between different aims. Securing, for example, higher rates of employment and higher productivity in economically lagging regions not only brings national efficiency gains but can increase the general standard of living and social welfare in such regions and thereby achieve greater spatial equity of opportunities and outcomes (Martin 2008).

As shown in Chap. 3, Sect. 3.2, if a weight is attached to each region, then policies of investment allocation may result in a high growth of the economy as a whole and reduce income asymmetries between regions. Such conclusions, however, are tentative since the objective function, associated with the process of regional allocation of investment, is focused on maximising national income. Regional policy, however, may be seen not only as a redistributive policy shifting resources from rich to poor regions but also as a policy aimed at improving growth at the national level. This was formulated by Michel et al. (1983) in terms of a trade-off function. This model, however, incurs the possibility of a prolonged period of severe regional inequalities (the phase of 'autonomous' development). Moreover, Michel et al. (1983) set an unrealistic aim, namely, absolute regional equality. The issue is to minimise regional inequalities in such a way as to allow the entire economy to operate in a more efficient way. Chinitz (1966) puts forward the essence of this argument by asking if 'any effort to stimulate growth in particular regions can be *compatible* with a national growth policy' (p. 1) [emphasis added]. Chinitz (1966) presents the argument in a verbal way. A by-product of this study, therefore, is to express this argument in a precise mathematical way.

This chapter attempts to incorporate the possibility of compatibility in aims of regional policy in a framework of regional allocation of investment, using the well-established mathematical method of OCT. Following this introduction, this chapter is divided into five sections. Section 4.2 aims at exploring the various meanings of regional equity and aggregate efficiency. Based on an alternative notion of 'regional equity', developed in Sect. 4.2, the argument of compatibility between regional equity and aggregate efficiency is extended further by developing a set of optimal regional policies (Sect. 4.3). Section 4.4 considers two modelling aspects that have important implications for policy-making, namely, optimal allocation policies in a multiregional economy and the incorporation of sectoral elements in the analysis of optimal regional policies. Some key points about the use of this framework in regional planning along with the process of evaluating regional policy are included in Sect. 4.5. The final section concludes by reflecting on some of the key implications of the model.

4.2 Redefining the Aim of 'Regional Equity'

The assertion of a trade-off between 'equity' and 'efficiency' is little more than an attitude of mind, until one defines these terms (Osberg 1995). 'Regional equity' and 'aggregate efficiency' should be defined in such a way in order to reflect reality, permitting, at the same time, the specification of regional policies that allow improving the regional distribution of income without reducing the rate of growth of the economy as a whole. These 'conceptual complexities' are discussed in this section.

The notion of 'efficiency' can be used as a criterion in judging how well markets have allocated resources or as the maximum production that can be obtained given the resources available (Baldassari and Piga 1996). There is also the notion of technical efficiency. Following Sen (1975), a situation can be described as technically efficient if it is 'impossible to move to an alternative such that the change yields something for nothing' (p. 13). Such definition is, in fact, a weak criterion of economic performance (Sen 1975). A more efficient society can produce more with the same amount of resources—a definition close to the original argument by Okun (1975). 'Efficiency' is an ambiguous notion and has many meanings to regional policy (Vanhove and Klaasen 1980). Trevo (1989), for example, defines 'efficiency' in terms of growth maximisation in real GDP. This definition seems to be in accordance with the structure of the model of regional allocation of investment, which makes it appropriate to the aims of this study.

Turning to the second aim of regional policy, 'equity' is a slippery concept and several popular notions compete for attention (Reiner 1965); equal opportunities, participation in the decision-making process and so on can be mentioned indicatively. Is regional equity a matter of equal regional growth rates, or one of an equal share in benefits of growth? Is 'regional equity' achieved with no further aggravation of present interregional inequalities, or is it tantamount to the eradication of such differences in well-being?[1] Such features do not seem to provide an adequate basis for designing optimal regional policies until they are transformed into a single variable. In addition, there is the issue of incorporating qualitative and quantitative features into the same aim. The quantitative aspect requires that the aim should be expressed in specific measurable variable, easily grasped by citizens and policy-makers.

'Regional equity' is usually defined as a condition in which all regions within a nation have approximately equal values for a quantitative indicator of the standard of living or equivalent levels of opportunity, economic and social benefit, cost and risk (Goodall 1987). Following this definition, an obvious candidate to approximate 'regional equity' is absolute interregional equality in terms of per capita income at a pre-specified terminal time. Using the notation introduced in Chap. 3, this proxy can be expressed as $G_{1,2}(T) = 0$. A policy of equalising regional disparities is, however, unrealistic and would involve considerable sacrifices in terms of national growth (aggregate efficiency). As Kenworthy (1995) notes 'achieving complete distributive equality would virtually eliminate monetary incentives, which surely would subsequently reduce work effort and investment' (p. 228). Growth in the geographical scale is axiomatically uneven, and by definition, relative improvements cannot be shared by all. Complete equity in regional incomes might remain in equilibrium in a stagnating economy, and once growth is initiated again disequilibrium will be established. It might prove more instructive to develop a more pragmatic, and feasible, proxy of 'regional equity'. In order to give a still different perspective to the problem of regional allocation of investment, one further step should be taken. A key question is whether the economic or social conditions that they represent are of a scale or severity that justifies intervention. Consider a finite time horizon, let $[t_0 \ldots T]$, and adopt 'intervention logic', namely, that there is an initial level of interregional disparities that justify policy intervention, let $G_{1,2}(t_0)$. Arrow (1979) defines 'equity' in terms of 'as much equality of income as is possible'. In this sense, 'regional equity' requires that interregional disparities should be gradually lessened period by period or to narrow the income gap: an aim reflected by the condition $G_{1,2}(t) \to 0$ as $t \to T$, which implies 'minimisation of interregional disparities'. 'Regional equity' can be specified further as a 'tolerable' level of interregional disparities (or an 'acceptable' boundary) at a terminal time. Denote this 'acceptable' boundary as $\bar{G}_{1,2}(T)$, then 'regional equity' can be approximated as $\bar{G}_{1,2}(T) < G_{1,2}(t_0)$: an aim more 'palatable politically and perhaps 'the most that a reasonable politician could demand' (Reiner 1965, p. 116).[2]

Turning to the definition of 'aggregate efficiency', as argued earlier, this is in fact a policy question and a bit closer to policy prescriptions. It reflects how much 'leakage' a society is willing to accept in order to achieve a certain level of 'regional equity'. Stewart and Streeten (1976) argue that equity 'is an important end in itself, and some would be prepared to accept reductions in average levels, and even, up to a point, in all levels of income, to achieve greater equality' (p. 383). Having this argument in mind, 'aggregate efficiency' can be reflected in terms of an 'accepted' level of national income, let $\bar{Y}_N(T)$, with the additional constraint that $\bar{Y}_N(T) > Y_N(t_0)$. The 'dual' aim of $\bar{G}_{1,2}(T)$ and $\bar{Y}_N(T)$ can be considered as 'ex-ante conditionality' or the 'thematic goal' of regional policy.[3]

The definitions proposed in this section can also be seen as a set of 'milestones', a mean of monitoring progress towards achievement of the milestones, and a plan for revision of activities according to observed results (Blakely 1994). This is a kind of model, or more accurately, a methodological perspective that can be used to give precise answers to specific questions.

Choosing an allocation policy that maximises national income, but without exceeding a predetermined gap, might be a rational way to tackle with the 'dilemma' of regional policy: a technocratic and socially feasible solution. The scope, therefore, for reducing interregional inequalities is not incompatible with improvements in aggregate efficiency. There is, as Baldassari and Piga (1996) argue, 'considerable room to demonstrate that equity and efficiency can be *synergic*, that is, there is a phase of improvement of the conditions of equity which cause greater accumulation and hence greater economic growth' (p. 259). Once this knowledge is introduced, the objective function appears as $\max_{\delta} Z$, where the term $Z = \bar{Y}_N(T) - \varphi \bar{G}_{1,2}(T)$ can be interpreted as a 'trade-off' function. Instead of applying a partial allocation at each point in time, the 'fund' is allocated exclusively to one region, which implies the following allocation constraint

$$0 \le \delta \le 1 \tag{4.1}$$

Using this constraint, the phase of autonomous development, which as argued in Chap. 3 might perpetuate regional inequalities, can be avoided. Adopting an 'exclusive' allocation parameter, capital in each region accumulates according to the following relationships:

$$\dot{K}_1 = \delta S_N \tag{4.2}$$

$$\dot{K}_2 = (1 - \delta) S_N \tag{4.3}$$

In keeping with the spirit of the production relationship, introduced in Chap. 2, Sect. 2.3, the target function to be optimised is expressed as $\underset{\delta}{\text{Max}}\left\{\left[v_1K_1(T)+v_2K_2(T)\right]-\varphi\left[v_1K_1(T)-v_2K_2(T)\right]\right\}$, subject to the constraints (4.1), (4.2) and (4.3).

The associated Hamiltonian function, $H=[\delta(p_1-p_2)+p_2](\gamma_1K_1+\gamma_2K_2)$, implies that the ad-joint conditions are similar to those developed in Chap. 2. Thus, $\dot{p}_1=-\left[\delta(p_1-p_2)+p_2\right]\gamma_1$ and $\dot{p}_2=-\left[\delta(p_1-p_2)+p_2\right]\gamma_2$. The objective function, proposed in this section, however, implies different terminal conditions. Specifically, $P_1(T)=v_1(1-\varphi)$ and $P_2(T)=v_2(1+\varphi)$.

While the ad-joint conditions imply similar allocation criteria for the initial time, the objective function adopted here alters the criteria for the optimal allocation at the terminal time. Why this is so, it can be seen from the following relationship: $P_1(T)-P_2(T)=\{[(v_1-v_2)-(v_1+v_2)\varphi]/[v_2(1+\varphi)]\}P_2(T)$.

Of particular importance is the 'weight' attached to the aim of 'regional equity'. While $\varphi<0$ does not make any economic sense, setting $\varphi=0$, then $Z=Y_N(T)$, implying that optimal policies improve only the growth of the economy as a whole. A high-growth policy, however, as Stewart and Streeten (1976) note 'tends not only to generate inequalities, but also to establish positions of power that makes extremely difficult to combat those inequalities by government redistributive policies, and indeed make it likely that anti-egalitarian policies will be adopted' (p. 393). Obviously, a meaningful objective function applicable to the dilemma of regional policy requires not only $\varphi\neq0$ but also $\varphi>0$.[4]

At this juncture, it is important to note that the value of φ is to a great extent subjective, blended by a personal set of interests and preferences.[5] In other words, φ is politically highly sensitive. Any researcher in regional economics and any worker in policy-making are keenly aware of the pressures originating mainly from political circles. The weight attached to the aim of 'regional equity' can be considered as a way to portray political considerations, which as will be explained below shape the pattern of regional allocation of investment. The value imposed to φ, thus, is tightly related to the institutional setting of the economy. Having this in mind, it is assumed that government has at least some concern for equity, implying $\varphi>0$. Assume that $\varphi=1$, then $P_1(T)=0$ and $P_2(T)=2v_2$, implying $P_1(T)-P_2(T)<0$. Obviously, if $\varphi=1$ then the fund at the terminal time is *always* allocated to the relatively poor region. By definition, however, the government has a concern for both 'regional equity' and 'aggregate efficiency'. As $\phi \to 0$, a greater interest is placed upon efficiency, whereas as $\phi \to 1$, a greater interest is placed upon 'regional equity'. It follows, therefore, that $\varphi \in]01[$. Introducing φ in the objective function provides a set of regional policies with attention to social and ethical aspects of economics, which will be examined in more detail in Sect. 4.3.

4.3 Overcoming the Dilemma of Regional Policy

Chinitz (1966) argues that 'if investment is relevant to growth, and if certain kinds of impediments to growth are regional in character, then a regionally stratified programme of investment may contribute to national growth' (p. 8). An allocation (regional) policy, therefore, at a given instance of time has two effects. It influences the rate of growth of national income and the degree of regional inequalities. A policy to reduce regional disparities is not only desirable on grounds of social justice, but in the long run, given certain conditions, is consistent with maximising national output. This 'development balance' can be encapsulated in terms of the following definition.

Definition Complementarities in regional policy at a predetermined terminal time, T, require $\partial Y_N/\partial t > 0 \wedge \partial G_{1,2}/\partial t < 0 \forall t \in [t_0 \ldots T]$ as a necessary condition, while $Y_N(t) \to \bar{Y}_N(T) \wedge G_{1,2}(t) \to \bar{G}_{1,2}(T)$ is a sufficient condition.

Propositions 1 and 2 describe optimal allocation policies, in accordance with this definition.

Proposition 1 If $G_{1,2}(t_0) > 0 \wedge \gamma_1 > \gamma_2$, then $\delta^*(t) = 1$ at $t_0 \leq t < T \wedge \delta^*(t) = 0$ at $t = T$.

Proof $\because \gamma_1 > \gamma_2$, the ad-joining conditions imply that $\delta^*(t) = 1$ at $t_0 \leq t < T$. As $\phi \to 1$, $\partial[P_1(t) - P_2(t)]/\partial t < 0$, provided that this condition holds $\forall t \in]t_0\ T]$, then $P_1(T) - P_2(T) < 0$ as $t \to T$. $\therefore \delta^*(t) = 0$ at $t = T$, irrespective if $v_1/v_2 > 1 \vee v_1/v_2 < 1$. Q.E.D.

Proposition 2 If $G_{1,2}(t_0) > 0 \wedge \gamma_1 < \gamma_2$, then $\delta^*(t) = 0$, $\forall t \in [t_0 \ldots T]$.

Proof $\because \gamma_1 < \gamma_2$, given the ad-joining conditions $\delta^*(t) = 0$ at $t_0 \leq t < T$. As $\varphi \to 1$ $\partial[P_1(t) - P_2(t)]/\partial t < 0$; consequently at $P_1(T) - P_2(T) < 0$, even if $v_1 < v_2 \vee v_1 > v_2; \therefore \delta^*(t) = 0 \forall t \in [t_0 \ldots T]$. Q.E.D.

Table 4.1 Allocation matrix: $G_{1,2}(t_0) > 0$; $\gamma_1 > \gamma_2$

	$v_1 > v_2, s_1 > s_2$	$v_1 < v_2, s_1 > s_2$
$\delta^*(t)$ at $t_0 \leq t < T$	1	1
$\delta^*(t)$ at $t = T$	0	0

Table 4.2 Allocation matrix: $G_{1,2}(t_0) > 0$; $\gamma_1 < \gamma_2$

	$v_1 > v_2, s_1 < s_2$	$v_1 < v_2, s_1 < s_2$
$\delta^*(t)$ at $t_0 \leq t < T$	0	0
$\delta^*(t)$ at $t = T$	0	0

Propositions 1 and 2 indicate that $P_1(T) - P_2(T) < 0 \ \forall t \in [t_0 \ldots T]$, irrespective of the ratio v_1/v_2. Provided that $\partial[P_1(T) - P_2(T)]/\partial\varphi < 0$, then the sign of the term $[P_1(T) - P_2(T)]$ is determined, essentially, by the value attached to φ.

Tables 4.1 and 4.2 set out the optimal allocation policies implied by Propositions 1 and 2.

Assume that $\gamma_1 > \gamma_2$ and $v_1 > v_2$. Initially, the fund is allocated to region 1, in accordance with the aim of aggregate efficiency. The weight attached to equity, however, implies that $P_1(T) - P_2(T) < 0$; therefore, $\delta^*(t) = 0$ at $t = T$.[6] According to the analysis in Chap. 2, if $v_1 > v_2$, then the optimal policy at $t = T$ is $\delta^*(t) = 1$: a policy that sustains, and increases, regional inequalities. Introducing φ in the objective function, however, alters the pattern of the allocation policy in favour of the relatively poor region. The essence of this argument is illustrated in Fig. 4.1.

Before the switching point, national output evolves at an increasing rate, a condition that holds throughout the entire planning period: $\Upsilon_N(t) \rightarrow \Upsilon_N(T)$, $\partial\Upsilon_N/\partial t > 0 \forall t \in [t_0 \ldots T]$. On the other hand, $\partial G_{1,2}/\partial t > 0$ holds $\forall t \in [t_0 \ldots t^*)$. A 'switch' in the allocation parameter at time $t = t^*$ induces a declining tendency in interregional inequalities at a rate approximating $\{[G_{1,2}(T) - G_{1,2}(t^*)]/G_{1,2}(t^*)\}/(T - t^*)$. Due to the switch in δ at $t = t^*$, $G_{1,2} = \bar{G}_{1,2}$ at $t = T$: a condition consistent with the aim of 'regional equity'. During the interval $]t^* \ldots T]$, national output and the gap in regional incomes evolve towards different directions, that is, $\partial\Upsilon_N/\partial t > 0$ and $\partial G_{1,2}/\partial t < 0$. Provided that these two conditions hold $\forall t \in]t^* \ldots T]$, then $\Upsilon_N(t_0) - \Upsilon_N(T) < 0$ and $G_{i,2}(t_0) - G_{1,2}(T) > 0$.[7] On the other hand, during the period $[t_0 \ldots t^*]$, there is a transitory (or temporary) 'trade-off', as

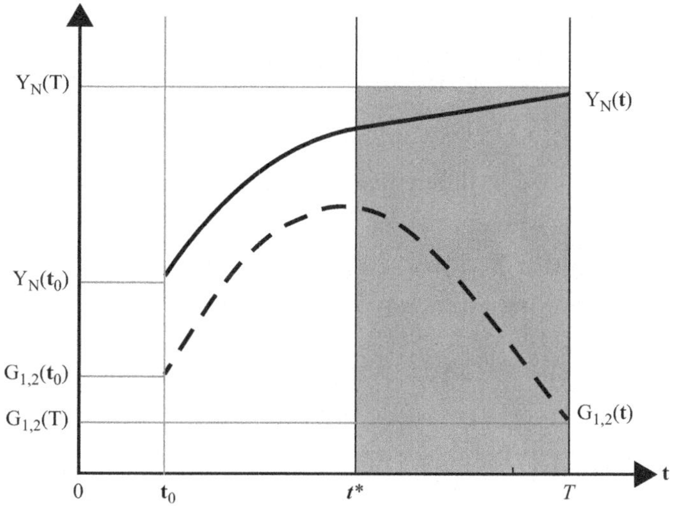

Fig. 4.1 Optimal allocation: $\gamma_1 > \gamma_2$; $G_{1,2}(t_0) > 0$

indicated by the conditions $\partial G_{1,2}/\partial t > 0$ and $\partial \Upsilon_N/\partial t > 0 \forall t \in [t_0 \ldots t^*)$. This situation, nonetheless, can be restored at $]t^* \ldots T]$ due to the properties of the system.

As argued in Chap. 3, an objective function concentrated *exclusively* on aggregate efficiency (i.e. setting $\varphi = 0$), in conjunction with the conditions $\gamma_1 > \gamma_2$ and $v_1 > v_2$, perpetuates 'inherited' regional inequalities. Setting the condition $\varphi \in]0\,1[$ and a limit on interregional disparities reverses this situation and both aims are compatible. If the level of national income obtained by a policy of 'concentrated' regional growth is higher relative to that obtained by a 'distribution' policy, then a trade-off is evident. Assume, however, that underutilised sources in the poor region are activated as a result of a policy switching the allocation parameter. In this case, a relatively higher national income can be obtained.

As it can be seen from Fig. 4.1, $\Upsilon_N(t), \forall t \in [t_0 \ldots t^*) < \Upsilon_N(t), \forall t \in [t^* \ldots T]$ or $[\Upsilon_N(T) - \Upsilon_N(t^*)]/(T - t^*) > [\Upsilon_N(t^*) - \Upsilon_N(t_0)]/(t^* - t_0)$. This condition provides support to the argument that persisting regional inequalities are in fact nationally inefficient.

At this point, it is worth mentioning that φ alters the switching time. To be more specific, the rate of inter-temporal change in p_i is defined as $[p_1(t) - P_1(T)]/[p_2(t) - P_2(T)] = p_1(t)/p_2(t)$. Given the ad-joint and the terminal conditions, it follows that $[p_1(t)-v_1(1-\varphi)]/[p_2(t)-v_2(1+\varphi)]=\gamma_1/\gamma_2$, implying $p_1-p_2=[(\gamma_1-\gamma_2)/\gamma_2]p_2+[(v_1v_2)/\gamma_2][s_2(1-\varphi)-s_s(1+\varphi)]$; solving for p_1 yields $p_1=(\gamma_1/\gamma_2)p_2+[(v_1v_2)/\gamma_2][s_2(1-\varphi)-s_s(1+\varphi)]$. Setting $p_1=p_2^*$ gives $p_2^*=(v_1v_2)\{[s_1(1+\varphi)-s_2(1-\varphi)]/(\gamma_1-\gamma_2)\}$. Given that $\dot{p}_2=-p_2\gamma_2$, then $\dot{p}_2+p_2\gamma_2=0$: a differential equation with the general solution $p_2(t)=Ae^{\gamma_2(T-t)}$, where A is an arbitrary constant. Setting $t=T$, then $p_2(T)=A$; given that $P_2(T)=v_2(1+\varphi)$, then $p_2(t)=v_2(1+\varphi)e^{\gamma_2(T-t)}$. Since $p_1=p_2^*$, the following expression can be obtained:

$$v_2(1+\varphi)e^{\gamma_2(T-t)}=(v_1v_2)\{[s_1(1+\varphi)-s_2(1-\varphi)]/(\gamma_1-\gamma_2)\} \tag{4.4}$$

Solving Eq. (4.4) for t gives the switching time of δ:

$$t_\varphi^*=T-1/\gamma_2\log\{v_1[s_1(1+\varphi)-s_2(1-\varphi)]/[(\gamma_1-\gamma_2)(1+\varphi)]\} \tag{4.5}$$

Comparing Eq. (4.5) with the expression for the switching time (t^*), derived in Chap. 2, Sect. 2.4, it can be easily shown that $T-t^*>T-t_\varphi^*$. If $\varphi=0$, then $t_\varphi^*\equiv t^*$. On the other hand, for $\varphi\approx 1$, or more accurately for the set of policies implied when $\varphi\to 1$, $t_\varphi^*<t^*$.

It is reasonable to assume that the behaviour of agents varies *systematically* with changes in policy.[8] If $\gamma_1>\gamma_2$ and $v_1>v_2$, then improving v_2 and s_2 reduces the transition period. If $\gamma_1>\gamma_2$ and $v_1<v_2$, then improvements of s_2 have a similar impact upon the switching time.

Consider the time sequence of optimal regional allocation of investment over a long-run time horizon, let $[t_0\ldots\ T_0]_0\cdots[t_n\ldots T_n]_n$. Assume further that $G_{1,2}(T)\neq\bar{G}_{1,2}$ at $t=T_0$. If $v_1<v_2$ $\forall t\in[t_1\ldots T_1]$, with $t_1>T$, then $\varphi\in\,]0\,1]$ implies that $\delta^*(t)=0$. This policy can be applied until $G_{1,2}(T)=\bar{G}_{1,2}$, depending on the changes in an agent's behaviour, which can be reflected in the elasticity of t_φ^* with respect to changes in the propensity to save and the productivity of capital. Similarly, $\delta^*(t)=1$ at $T<t_1<T_1$ and $\delta^*(t)=0$ at $t=T_1$ when $v_1>v_2$. Essentially, this procedure describes a multi-annual programming periods. An approach based on the value of φ provides a more stable policy environment, allowing strategic coordination and helps to avoid wasteful and irrational spending.

A case of particular interest is when the relatively poor region grows at a rate higher compared to that of the relatively rich region, namely, when $\gamma_1 - \gamma_2 < 0$. This is a clear case of overcoming the trade-off in the aims of regional policy. Here, the optimal policy is $\delta^* = 0 \forall t \in [t_0 \ldots T]$. The intuition behind this argument can be illustrated geometrically by Fig. 4.2.

It should be visible in Fig. 4.2 that $\partial Y_N / \partial t > 0$ and $\partial G_{1,2}/\partial t < 0$, $\forall t \in [t_0 \ldots T]$, while at $t = T$, $Y_N(t_0) - Y_N(T) < 0$ and $G_{i,2}(t_0) - G_{1,2}(T) > 0$. If $\gamma_1 < \gamma_2$, then $\delta^*(t) = 0 \forall t \in [t_0 \ldots T]$, *irrespective* of the ratio v_1/v_2. Placing greater emphasis on regional equity, therefore, does not allow interregional inequalities to increase, as implied by $\delta^*(t) = 1$ at $t_0 \leq t < T$ and $\delta^*(t) = 0$ at $t = T$. It is worthy to highlight here that such conclusions are valid as long as the value attached to φ sustains the condition $(v_1 - v_2) < (v_1 + v_2)$.

Consider an initial situation in which $G_{2,1}(t_0) > 0$. The objective function in this case is $\max_{\delta}\left[Y_N(T) - \varphi\bar{G}_{2,1}(T)\right]$, with $0 < \bar{G}_{2,1}(T) < G_{2,1}(t_0)$. Maintaining OCT as the basic vehicle of analysis, $\gamma_1 > \gamma_2$ implies $\delta^*(t) = 1$ at

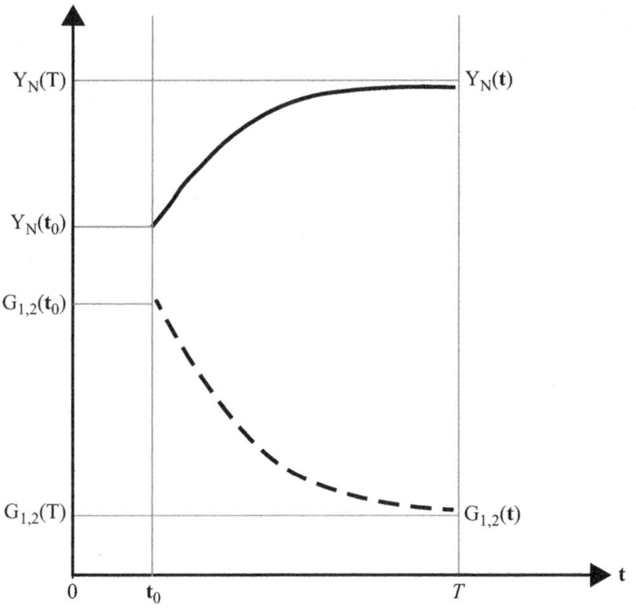

Fig. 4.2 Optimal allocation: $\gamma_1 < \gamma_2$; $G_{1,2}(t_0) > 0$

$t_0 \leq t < T$ and $\delta^*(t) = 0$ if $\gamma_1 < \gamma_2$. The terminal conditions $P_1(T) = v_1(1+\varphi)$ and $P_2(T) = v_2(1-\varphi)$ imply

$$P_1(T) - P_2(T) = \left\{\left[(v_1 - v_2) + (v_1 + v_2)\varphi\right] / \left[v_2(1-\varphi)P_2(T)\right]\right\} \quad (4.6)$$

Given that $(v_1 - v_2) < (v_1 + v_2)$ and $(v_1 - v_2) + (v_1 + v_2)\varphi > 0$, then $P_1(T) - P_2(T) > 0$: a critical condition for choosing the allocation policy at the terminal time. Tables 4.3 and 4.4 set out the optimality conditions for $\gamma_1 > \gamma_2$ and $\gamma_1 < \gamma_2$, respectively.

A swift glance at Tables 4.3 and 4.4 reveals that the set of policies implied by $G_{2.1}(t_0) > 0$ is, in fact, a 'mirror' image of the policies implied by $G_{1,2}(t_0) > 0$. Let $\gamma_1 - \gamma_2 > 0$. According to Table 4.3, $\delta^*(t) = 1, \forall t \in [t_0 \ldots T]$, irrespective of the v_i/v_j ratio. Both Υ_N and $G_{2,1}$ follow a path similar to that in Fig. 4.2. A case of particular interest is when $\gamma_1 - \gamma_2 < 0$. According to Table 4.4, the optimal policy is $\delta^*(t) = 0$ at $t_0 \leq t < T$ and $\delta^*(t) = 1$ at $t = T$. As $t \rightarrow t^*$ allocating the fund in region 2 implies $\partial G_{2.1}/\partial t < 0$ and $\partial \Upsilon_N/\partial t > 0$. At the time segment $[t_0 \ldots t^*)$, there is compatibility in aims, while at $[t_0 \ldots T]$, the policy $\delta^* = 1$ results in $\partial \Upsilon_N/\partial t > 0$ and $\partial G_{2.1}/\partial t > 0$. A switch in δ, therefore, improves 'aggregate efficiency' at the expanse of 'regional equity'. Why this should be so is clear from Fig. 4.3.

In Fig. 4.2, a trade-off is evident at $[t_0 \ldots t^*]$, while Fig. 4.3 indicates a trade-off *after* the 'switch' in δ. At $[t^* \ldots T]$, $\Upsilon_N(t_0) < \Upsilon_N(T)$ accompanied with an increasing tendency in interregional inequalities. Nevertheless, this policy implies $G_{2.1}(t_0) > G_{2.1}(T)$, which is equivalent to 'minimising' the trade-off. Incorporating regional inequalities in the objective function instead of as an additional constraint, promotes both 'regional equity' and

Table 4.3 Allocation matrix: $G_{2,1}(t_0) > 0$; $\gamma_1 > \gamma_2$

	$v_1 > v_2, s_1 > s_2$	$v_1 < v_2, s_1 > s_2$
$\delta^*(t)$ at $t_0 \leq t < T$	1	1
$\delta^*(t)$ at $t = T$	1	1

Table 4.4 Allocation matrix: $G_{2,1}(t_0) > 0$; $\gamma_1 < \gamma_2$

	$v_1 > v_2, s_1 < s_2$	$v_1 < v_2, s_1 < s_2$
$\delta^*(t)$ at $t_0 \leq t < T$	0	0
$\delta^*(t)$ at $t = T$	1	1

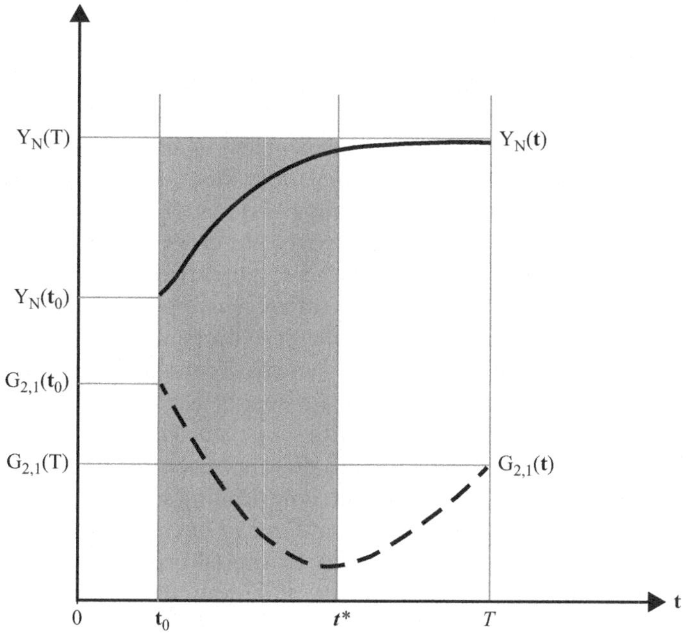

Fig. 4.3 Optimal allocation: $\gamma_1 < \gamma_2$; $G_{2.1}(t_0) > 0$

'aggregate efficiency'. Regional development policy, therefore, is not only a social and political necessity but a fundamental part of a (broad) policy to promote national economic growth. Similarly, if maximisation of national output is not considered as constraint, it assists the aim of 'regional equity'. In other words, there is a 'feed-back' relation between 'regional equity' and 'aggregate efficiency'.

Investing in the initially poor region helps to avoid negative externalities from additional accumulation of capital or congestion from concentration of activities in the initially rich region and simultaneously enabling the lagging region to enjoy a relatively high rate of growth. Alternatively, the switch in the allocation parameter may take place when policy-makers realise that further accumulation of capital might cause negative externalities in a region characterised by a relatively high level of productivity, which can be considered as a case of overcoming the trade-off in the aims of regional policy.

Nevertheless, another point deserves notice at this juncture. The allocation policies set out in Table 4.4 imply that the period during which a trade-off between regional equity and aggregate efficiency takes place will be smaller *if* region 1 improves both s_1 and v_1. Taking into account the various institutional constraints, it is reasonable to assume that the behaviour (or attitude) of agents (individuals, organisations and government) varies with changes in policy. Following a switch in δ, therefore, the values of s and/or v can be changed (or improved) in order to reflect a spectrum of possible policy responses, which lead to an entirely different (possibly more advanced and efficient) path of transformation, essentially a process towards an advanced stage of economic development.

Attention should be drawn to the fact that regional economies should not be highly dependent on financial assistance. The model in this section might give the impression that describes a permanently dependent economy. Continuous reliance on the fund does not promote economic development in the long run. This, however, is misleading since the *intraregional* policies to improve the propensity to save in conjunction with programmes aiming to advances in the productivity of capital provide a safeguard. In the long run, improvements in those structural characteristics will help regions to avoid reliance on the 'fund'.

Several of the policies advocated here have to be modified according to the responses of the society. The structure of the system discussed in this section has an important property. In particular, it describes a system that not only detects optimal regional policies but also it provides an *endogenous* mechanism which allows to adapt to the situation or conditions created by the function of the system itself. This is plainly clear when the lagging region receives the fund sooner, that is, when t_{φ}^{*} is reduced due to efforts of the lagging region to improve capital productivity during the period before the switch (which are intentional in order to receive the fund in the next period) or when this region receives the fund, due to the value attached to the aim of 'regional equity', but improves the growth rate or the propensity to save as a result of this policy. In short, the analysis in this section provides support to the argument that shifts in saving behaviour and by extension in investment, induced by redistribution accompanied by changes in attitudes assist the implementation of development policies.

A concern for policy conflicts is reflected by the provisions of article 175 of the EU Treaty,[9] which mentions that member states should coordinate their economic policies so as to attain the objectives set out in article 174. The structure of the model can be applied to EU in the context of Cohesion Policy in order to avoid 'poor targeting', one of the major concerns in the EU. The process of decision-making, developed here, applies tangible criteria based on structural characteristic of regional economies (i.e. the propensity to save and capital productivity). In contrast, with simple statistical criteria (e.g. a percentage of the average income in the EU), such criteria indicate the growth prospects of regions which contribute to the economic development of the EU as a whole. A key question is whether Cohesion Policy should be embedded within a wider policy framework with a view to achieving policy coherence with other relevant policies at both EU and national levels. The model in this section is in position to provide some guidelines towards that aim since it explicitly establishes a link between the overall (national or supranational) and the regional level (encapsulated in the variable reflecting the gap in regional incomes). As Bachtler et al. (2003) argue, regional policy in the EU cannot be viewed simply from a national perspective. Instead, there is a need to take into account the interrelationships between national regional policies, EU regional policy and EU competition policy, a policy that predates Cohesion Policy by several decades. As Wishlade and Michie (2009) note

> the scope for conflict was clearly recognised in the 1988 Structural Funds reforms under which the Regulation 2052/88 specified that the Funds should comply with completion policy. Nevertheless, while EU Cohesion policy explicitly intervenes to alter economic outcomes, EU Competition policy aims to ensure that State intervention does not interfere with the smooth functioning of the internal market or distort completion to an extent contrary to the common interest, which may cause serious conflicts.

The notion of the 'fund', proposed in this study, can be used as a basis for further discussion of EU fiscal capacity. Mendez and Bachtler (2015) suggest that member states agree on overall policy objectives for the EU and a politically acceptable net balance (i.e. what they are prepared to contribute to the EU budget), and then subsequently decisions would be made on how the funding is to be spent to meet the policy objectives. The approach in this chapter sets policy objectives as an acceptable level of aggregate output, which is an essential component of the competitiveness of an economy, while the criteria for optimal allocation of the fund may change according to the value of the weight attached to regional equity. This is to say that in a multi-annual period, policy-makers may impose either $\varphi \rightarrow 1$ or $\varphi \rightarrow 0$, depending on the level of regional gap in each period. This framework, therefore, may help the overarching goals of Cohesion Policy and the EU fiscal consolidation, in conjunction with an effective administration of respective funds.

Essentially, the approach outlined in this section implies a shift towards a more integrated approach, in which regional development policy is not only a social and political necessity but a fundamental part of a policy to promote competitiveness of the economy as a whole. A decision-maker who seeks to overcome the trade-off in the aims of regional policy by experimenting with different values of the weight attached to 'regional equity' and modifying the main parameters, according to the characteristics of each region, can generate a wide range of policies.

However, it seems too optimistic to hope that the adoption of this policy by itself, without structural improvements in the administrative agencies of the government would increase national income and improve 'regional equity'. There is a major long-standing issue: the continuing and mutually weak liaison and understanding between researchers and the decision takers or policy-makers, stemming from lack of communication among people working in parallel. Additionally, in any economic organisation, agents differ with respect to their possibilities of action, their initial information and their preferences. This is not a matter of institutions (or innovation in institutions), but how they are run, who runs them and what they want. House (1973) argues that this may be a shortcoming on the part of researchers, ill-trained academically for problem-solving or action orientation in an operational role, or it may result from an inadequacy on the part of decision takers to appreciate the potential offered by individual disciplines, in either an academic or an applied context. Especially, at the regional level, an obstacle, according to House (1973), is the 'widespread inability or disinclination by administrators to view problems, decisions or policies in a spatial framework or even as having an important spatial implication' (p. 273).

Judgment permeates planning (Dakin 1963). There is a need to make these judgments reasonable, rational and defensible. The approach in this chapter fulfils these criteria and can be used in proposals for preparing regional development programmes. There exists no universal format for the preparation of strategic plans for regional development. Nevertheless, the decision-making process in this chapter can be applied in describing the content and structure of a strategic plan for regional development, with the necessary flexibility to adjust as conditions change (macro-conditionality policy-making). In this way, it can be seen as a framework that allows changes in the administrative/institutional (even inventing new) structures or improving poor administrative capacities, which is an obstacle in the economies of several lagging regions. This, however, requires an ability to accept and incorporate new knowledge and ideas. There is a need to change the behaviour and the concept of society and a person's position in it. Development, after all, 'implies *change* and this is one sense in which the term development is used' (Thirlwall 1994, p. 9) [emphasis added].

Nevertheless, in this stage another issue deserves particular attention. What sectoral policies should give more consideration to their territorial impact when being designed? What tools could be developed in this regard? Section 4.4 extends the results for an economy with *n*-regions, each characterised by the presence of different sectors, namely, a multiregional/sectoral economy. This extension adds more realism in the model by assisting the process of targeted investment when the focus is upon both regions and sectors.

4.4 Compatibility in the Aims of Regional Policy in a Multiregional/Multispectral Economy

Throughout this study, an economy with two regions is assumed. This setting may appear as restrictive. A 'region', however, is not only physical space or a section of a nation. It is a very generalised and flexible concept (Isard 1956). Taking this argument into account, the model can be applied in various contexts. Just as an example, the model can also be applied for a single region, provided that can be divided into two distinct zones (e.g. urban and rural) or for sectors located in a given region (say an agricultural and an industrial area). Obviously, in this case, the focus is rather on intra-regional than interregional aspects of growth. Moreover, consider the distribution of the fund between two distinct groups of regions, say a group of 'agricultural' and another that includes 'industrial' regions or between geographically specified sets of regions, for example, 'northern' and 'southern' regions. Nevertheless, it is convenient to conduct the analysis in a multiregional economy with different sectors.

Consider an economy divided into a finite number of regions, n. In a multiregional economy, total (national) output can be approximated in terms of the following national accounting identity: $Y_N = \sum_{i=1}^{n} Y_i$. In this context, it seems legitimate to assume not only variations in regional incomes but also that there is a region in which per capita income exceeds per capita income in any other region. This region can be considered as the 'leading' region of the economy, denoted by the subscript L. This is a critical assumption for the analysis in this section, which can be expressed as $G_i \equiv (Y_L - Y_i)_t > 0$. It is also assumed that the 'leading' region sustains its position over a finite time horizon. This assumption is represented as $G_i(t) > 0 \; \forall t \in [t_0 \dots T]$. The basic relationships of the model can be described by the following set of equations: $Y_N = \sum_{i=1}^{n} v_i K_i$, $I_N = \sum_{i=1}^{n} \dot{K}_i$ and $S_N = \sum_{i=1}^{n} s_i Y_i$. Using this set, two relationships of particular importance can be obtained: $S_N = \sum_{i=1}^{n} s_i v_i K_i = \sum_{i=1}^{n} \gamma_i K_i$ and $\sum_{i=1}^{n} \dot{K}_i = \sum_{i=1}^{n} \gamma_i K_i$.

An allocation parameter (β_i) is attached to each region and capital accumulates accordingly as $\dot{K}_i = \beta_i S_N \; \forall i$. At any (discrete) point in time, that is, the following restriction is applied: $\sum_{i=1}^{n} \beta_i = 1$, $\forall t \in [t_0 \dots T]$ and $\forall i \neq L$.

'Aggregate efficiency' is defined as an accepted level of national output: $Y_N(t_0) - Y_N(T) < 0$. In a multiregional economy, 'regional equity' will be approximated as minimising the gap of *every* region with a 'leading region'. 'Regional equity', then, can be expressed in terms of the following general condition: $\sum_{i=1}^{m} G_i(t) \to 0$ as $t \to T$; $\forall i \neq L$ and $m < n$. What is, then, the appropriate modelling strategy in order to approximate the hypothesis of complementarities in the aims of regional policy? An insight is provided in a model by Ahluwalia and Chenery (1974). This model is developed specifically for the problem of maximising the weighted average of the rate of growth of the income of groups with different income levels. Ahluwalia and Chenery (1974) consider alternative strategies by imposing a weight equal to 1 to the poorest group and 1 to the other groups.[10] Modifying the objective function accordingly, a weight is attached to the income gap of each region with the leading region.[11] Thus, $\sum_{i=1}^{m} \varphi_i G_i$, with $\varphi_i \in]0 \;\, 1[$ $\forall i \neq L$. Taking into account the definition of 'aggregate efficiency', the next step follows on automatically. Thus,

$\underset{\delta}{Max}\, Z(T)$, where $Z = \sum_{i=1}^{n} Y_i(T) - \sum_{i=1}^{m} \varphi_i G_i(T)$, subject to the constraints $\beta_i \in [0\,1]$ and $\dot{K}_i = \beta_i(\gamma_1 K_1 + \dots + \gamma_L K_L + \dots + \gamma_n K_n) \; \forall i$.

Assuming that at each instant in time the fund is allocated only to one region,[12] the optimal solution is $\beta_j = 1$ and $\beta_i = 0, \forall i \neq j$. Given the Hamiltonian function $H = \sum_{i=1}^{n} \gamma_i K_i \sum_{i=1}^{n} p_i \beta_i$, the ad-joint conditions are defined as follows: $\dot{p}_i = -\partial H / \partial K_i = -\left(\sum_{i=1}^{n} p_i \beta_i \right) \gamma_i$.

In a multiregional economy, it is expected that $\gamma_1 < \ldots < \gamma_m$ and $v_1 < \ldots < v_m$. Assuming that regional disparities will always exist, which of the allocation policy should be chosen if the elements of regional policy, that is, 'regional equity' and 'aggregate efficiency', simultaneously enter within the ambit of a single aim?

The criterion for maximising the objective function at $0 \leq t < T$ is $\dot{p}_i / \dot{p}_j = \gamma_i / \gamma_j$. If $\gamma_i / \gamma_j < 1$, then $\beta_j^* = 1$ and $\beta_i^* = 0$. If, on the other hand, $\gamma_i / \gamma_j > 1$, then $\beta_i^* = 0$ and $\beta_j^* = 0$. At $t = T$, the criterion expressed in general terms is $P(T)_i / P(T)_j = v_i / v_j$. Consequently, if $v_i / v_j < 1$ ($v_i / v_j > 1$), then $\beta_j^* = 1$ and $\beta_i^* = 0$ ($\beta_i^* = 0$ and $\beta_j^* = 0$). Assuming that $\varphi_i \neq 0$, then $P_i(T) = \partial Z / \partial K_i = (1 + \varphi_i) v_i$, $\forall i \neq L$ and $p_L = \partial Z / \partial K_L = (1 - \varphi_1 - \ldots - \varphi_m) v_L$ for $i = L$. At $t = T$, therefore, the investment decision is made by applying the criterion $P_i(T) / P_L(T) = v_i / v_L$. The condition $p_L = (1 - \varphi_1 - \ldots - \varphi_m) v_L$ prevents from allocating the fund to the leading region at $t = T$. A region at which the fund is allocated at $t = T$ might be excluded in the subsequent period or when it reaches the predetermined boundary: $\bar{G}_j(T_i)$, with $T < T_i$. This process is repeated $\forall i \neq j$ and $\forall t \in]T_1 \ldots T_n]$, until the investment 'impulse', to use Keynesian jargon, helps every region to attain a 'tolerable' gap with the leading region.

In Chap. 2, the decision on allocating the fund is based upon the existing growth or productivity differentials across regions. Concentration of advanced and dynamic sectors in a region might account for these differentials. Assuming a substantial gap in regional incomes at an initial time, such policies can lead to perpetuation of regional inequalities—an argument put forward in Chap. 3. There is a necessity, therefore, to incorporate an element that explicitly accounts for the sectoral structure of the economy in each region.

In order to make the argument comprehensible, assume for the moment a two-region economy with two sectors in each region. Each sector possesses strategic structural and shift parameters through which they influence and are influenced by general activity[13]: an agricultural and a manufacturing sector, denoted by A and M, respectively. In terms of this notation, the simplest sectoral extension assumes that in the short run, production is subject to constant returns to scale, and production functions in each sector are governed by the assumption of proportionality. Thus, $Y_{i,j} = v_{i,j}K_{i,j}$, $\forall i = 1,2 \wedge j = A, M$. In constructing optimal regional/sectoral allocation policies, the framework described by $Y_i = \sum_j v_j K_j$, $Y_N = \sum v_{1j}K_{1j} + \sum v_{2j}K_{2j}$ or $Y_N = \sum v_{ij}K_{ij}$, $i = 1,2$; $j = A, M$ is used.

Although each sector is characterised by different propensities to save (i.e. $\Delta s_{ij} \neq 0$, $i = 1,2$; $j = A, M$), the savings behaviour is similar across sectors and regions. More specifically, a portion of output is saved by each sector for future consumption (investment): $S_{i,j} = s_{i,j}Y_{i,j}$; $S_i = \sum_j s_j v_j K_j$ and $S_N = \sum \gamma_{ij}K_{ij}$, where $\gamma_{ij} = v_{ij}s_{ij}$. Given that $\dot{K}_{ij} \equiv I_{ij} \equiv S_{ij}$, then $\dot{K}_N = \sum \gamma_{ij} K_{ij}$.

Introducing a sectoral perspective modifies the allocation parameter as $\delta = \sum \delta_{ij}$, or more specifically $\delta = \delta_{1A} + \delta_{1M} + \delta_{2A} + \delta_{2M}$, $i = 1,2$ and $j = A, M$: a parameter that simultaneously specifies which region and which sector will receive the fund. In other words, at each time period, the fund is allocated only to a particular region located in a specific region. In this sense, each allocation parameter reflects a policy measure that simultaneously accounts for regional/sectoral policy.

A policy-maker decides which sector/region will receive the fund comparing the differentials in the critical parameters, that is, $\Delta\gamma_{ij}$ and Δv_{ij}, $i = 1,2$; $j = A, M$. Consequently, at $0 \leq t < T$, the sector/region with the highest rate of growth receives the fund, that is, the corresponding allocation parameter is equal to 1 and 0 for the remaining sectors/regions. Similarly, at $t = T$, the value of the allocation parameter is equal to 1 for the region/sector with the highest capital productivity, while the remaining allocation parameters take a 0 value.

Capital in each region evolves according to $\dot{K}_{ij} = \delta_{ij}S_N$ $\forall ij$; assuming that government follows a regional/sectoral policy in order to maximise total output in the economy as a whole, then the objective function appears as $\max_{\delta_{ij}} \left[\sum_{j=A,M} v_{1,j}K_{1,j}(T) + \sum_{j=A,M} v_{2,j}K_{2,j}(T) \right]$.

The Hamiltonian function associated to the problem is expressed in the usual specification as $H = \sum p_{ij}\dot{K}_{ij}$. Taking into account, however, the allocation parameter and the relation that governs capital accumulation in each region/sector, the Hamiltonian is specified as follows:

$$H = \left(p_{1A}\delta_{1A} + p_{1M}\delta_{1M} + p_{2A}\delta_{2A} + p_{2M}\delta_{2M}\right)$$
$$\left(\gamma_{1A}K_{1A} + \gamma_{1M}K_{1M} + \gamma_{2A}K_{2A} + \gamma_{2M}K_{2M}\right)$$

The conditions for maximisation are $\dot{p}_{ij} = -\partial H / \partial K_{ij}$, implying $\dot{p}_{ij} = -A\gamma_{ij}$, where $A = (p_{1A}K_{1A} + p_{1M}K_{1M} + p_{2A}K_{2A} + p_{2M}K_{2M})$.

Deciding which region and which particular sector will receive the fund at $0 \leq t < T$ depends not only on the growth potentials of each region but also the growth characteristics of a particular sector, located in that region. Given the ad-joint conditions, therefore, a set of allocation criteria can be obtained. Thus, $p_{1M}(t)/p_{1A}(t) = \gamma_{1M}/\gamma_{1A}$, $p_{1M}(t)/p_{2M}(t) = \gamma_{1M}/\gamma_{2M}$, $p_{1M}(t)/p_{2A}(t) = \gamma_{1M}/\gamma_{2A}$, $p_{1A}(t)/p_{2M}(t) = \gamma_{1A}/\gamma_{2M}$, $p_{1A}(t)/p_{2A}(t) = \gamma_{1A}/\gamma_{2A}$ and $p_{2M}(t)/p_{2A}(t) = \gamma_{2M}/\gamma_{2A}$.

It stands to reason to assume that growth rates differ between sectors not only located in different regions but also for sectors that operate in the same region. Suppose, for example, that $\gamma_{1M} > \gamma_{1A} > \gamma_{2M} > \gamma_{2A}$. The optimality conditions imply that at the initial time the optimal allocation policy is $\delta^*_{1M} = 1 \wedge \delta^*_{ij} = 0 \, \forall ij \neq 1, M$. Given that $\Upsilon_N = \sum v_{ij}K_{ij}$, the terminal conditions are specified as $p_i(T) = \partial\Upsilon_N/\partial K_{ij} = v_{ij}$.

Optimality in the allocation policies at $t = T$ depends upon the sectoral/regional differential in capital productivity. Thus, $p_{1M}(T)/p_{1A}(T) = v_{1M}/v_{1A}$, $p_{1M}(T)/p_{2M}(T) = v_{1M}/v_{2M}$, $p_{1M}(T)/p_{2A}(T) = v_{1M}/v_{2A}$, $p_{1A}(T)/p_{2M}(T) = v_{1A}/v_{2M}$, $p_{1A}(T)/p_{2A}(T) = v_{1A}/v_{2A}$ and $p_{2M}(T)/p_{2A}(T) = v_{2M}/v_{2A}$.

It is logical to assume that capital productivity is also subject to a sectoral and regional degree of differentiation: $v_{1M} > v_{1A} > v_{2M} > v_{2A}$. Taking into account the terminal conditions, the optimal (regional/sectoral) allocation policy at $t = T$ is $\delta^*_{1M} = 1 \wedge \delta^*_{ij} = 0 \, \forall ij \neq 1, M$.

It is quite possible, however, such policies to intensify regional inequalities if the sector that will receive the fund is located in a relatively rich region at the initial time. Of course, a subsequent shift in the allocation parameter may alleviate the existing income inequalities, but such conclusion is only tentative. A 'trade-off' function that explicitly includes regional and sectoral considerations is necessary. Thus, $\max_{\delta_{ij}} \left\{ \sum_{j=A,M} v_{i,j}K_{i,j}(T) - \varphi\left[\sum_{j=A,M} v_{1,j}K_{1,j}(T) - \sum_{j=A,M} v_{2,j}K_{2,j}(T) \right] \right\}$, which can be extended for an economy with n-regions and m-sectors as follows:

$$\max_{\delta_{ij}} \left[\sum v_{i,j}K_{i,j}(T) - \sum \varphi_i G_{i,j}(T) \right],\ i = 1, \ldots n;\ j = 1, \ldots m.$$

At each instant in time, the fund is allocated only to one region/sector, given the existing differentials between regions (denoted by *i* and *j*) and sectors (indicated by the subscript *k* and *l*) in growth rates and capital productivity. For the purpose of programming optimal regional allocation policies, the foregoing points described earlier can be expressed more systematically by a set of optimality criteria. To be more specific, the optimality criteria at $0 \leq t < T$ are $\dot{p}_{i,k}(t)/\dot{p}_{i,l}(t) = \gamma_{i,k}/\gamma_{i,l}$, $\dot{p}_{i,k}(t)/\dot{p}_{j,k}(t) = \gamma_{i,k}/\gamma_{j,k}$ and $\dot{p}_{i,k}(t)/\dot{p}_{j,l}(t) = \gamma_{i,k}/\gamma_{j,l}$, while the same logic suggests that at $t = T$ optimal allocation is based on $P_{i,k}(T)/P_{i,l}(T) = v_{i,k}/v_{i,l}$, $P_{i,k}(T)/P_{j,k}(T) = v_{i,k}/v_{j,k}$ and $P_{i,k}(T)/P_{j,l}(T) = v_{i,k}/v_{j,l}$.

Imposing initial conditions for the sectors in each region, an allocation strategy is applied in order to combine regional and sectoral concerns, addressing issues of intraregional distribution of income, at least in an indirect way. Moreover, taking into account the weight of each region at the national and/or regional output or the contribution of each sector to regional employment and modifying the investment schemes accordingly, there is a gradual 'balance' between 'regional equity' and 'aggregate efficiency'.

It is important to note that the approach described in this chapter might be considered as a simplified one. A detailed model, however, may be difficult to be grasped and perhaps misleading, especially with day-to-day practise and experience in policy-making. Indeed, as Dasgupta and Hagger (1971) argue 'too much detailed may be self-defeating. A model with few hundred variables and several thousand possible alternatives can hardly provide a basis for a meaningful dialogue on optimum growth policies. Rather, it may well lead to what has sometimes been described as an "information death": one is killed by too much detail' (pp. 383–384). Despite its simplicity, the approach to the dilemma of regional policy developed in this chapter carries several important implications. Especially, in terms of implications for regional economic planning, the analysis in this section raises a number of pertinent issues given that regional policy is an element of planning for economic development at the national level and a mean through which the spatial dimension can be introduced into national government decision-making.

Following Chenery and Raduchel (1971), development planning originates as a response to the immobility and specificity of economic resources. It constitutes an attempt to 'improve on the allocation effects of market forces' (p. 29). Given this definition, it might be argued that the model in this chapter is relevant and applicable to development planning: 'an organised, intelligent attempt to select the best available alternatives to achieve specific goals' (Waterstone 1966, p. 8). Planning at the spatial level, especially, is concerned with the problem of coordination or integration of the spatial dimension of sectoral policies through a territorially based strategy (Cullingworth and Nadin 2006). Two conditions are required for rational regional planning (Haveman 1977). First, there must be knowledge of the effects of a policy on the lagging region and the other region. Second, it is essential that a trade-off function must be stipulated. The analysis in this chapter is based upon maximising an objective function that explicitly takes the possibility of a trade-off between regional equity and aggregate efficiency into account. By specifying initial conditions, the set of alternative allocation policies, developed in Sects. 4.3 and 4.4, can be considered as *investment plans* designed for specific regions, providing also an estimation of the effects of the proposed policy on the remaining regions in the economy. Obviously, such an approach can be particularly helpful to regional planning, as will be explained in Sect. 4.5.

4.5 Implications for Regional Planning

Is the unrestricted operation of the market economy compatible with the best interests of all society? The current recession, accompanied with persisting regional inequalities, is an indication that the 'market solution' may not be able to improve neither efficiency nor equity: a situation that makes an overwhelming case not only for government intervention but also for *development planning*, which sometimes taken as axiomatic, nevertheless, is generally made out in terms of the failings of an unregulated market economy (Killick 1976).[14] Development planning can be justified on several grounds, such as public goods (Moore 1978) and externalities (Evans 1974).[15] Any intervention aims to improve market efficiency, that is, when market does not result in a distribution of welfare under no one, can be made better off without someone else being made worse off (a Pareto optimum). Walker (1981) claims that '[...]markets failing to function in such a manner necessitate intervention into their operations in order to restore, or more closely approximate, optimality' (p. 268).

The choice, therefore, is not between 'planning' or 'not planning' but rather to what extent should there be (indicative) planning. An optimum 'mix' of planning and competition has to be specified. After all, planning is, as Todaro (1971) notes, 'a matter of degree' (p. 2), which accepts and complements markets. How much planning, on what scale and degree of complexity are questions which cannot be settled a priori; they must be discussed in the context of differing social backgrounds, the varying resource endowments, and the past performances and the future prospects of individual economies (countries or regions).

The exact meaning of 'planning' varies; it is a term with many meanings and can be conceived as a set of attempts to mobilise and channel resources to new or neglected uses, achieving on the process the legitimisation of new social objectives or a major realignment of existing objectives and as a process to scheme or arrange beforehand. Economic planning, therefore, can be defined as a 'programme of action' to provide for present and future demands including comprehensive statements of the objectives and policies which the government intends to pursue. The process of 'planning' involves normative choices and, according to De Melo et al. (1978), implies a desire to increase control over events, to reduce the realm of chance and to steer the economy onto a desired path. Planning might be described as macroeconomic management. Plans draw on resources to achieve goals or attempt to realise predetermined results or to consider the compatibility of desiderata (Pen 1965). Extending this definition, economic planning is the process of identifying an economy's future needs, together with systematic management of the scarce resources available in as efficient a manner as possible to satisfy those needs.

Most planning decisions can and should be made at the regional level. The approach developed in Sect. 4.3 sets specific goals (i.e. increasing output at the national level and reducing interregional inequalities) and provides a series of alternative policies to achieve these aims. To engage in economic development, a region must have the capacity to perform the function of economic planning through its local institutions. Regional planning is an important tool that helps agents (government or individuals) to make *optimal choices*. Economic planning at the regional level involves a method of procedure and has a vital role to play in confronting the contemporary problems faced by the developed and developing countries. Regional economic planning is a flexible tool, taking a variety of forms in response to problems that emerge in various contexts (Glasson 1992)[16] and can be incorporated into the planning of overall development policy. After all, spatial planning has a regulatory and a development function and is particularly important for countries in transition, since it can provide a way of managing and steering development, thereby creating a more stable climate for development and investment (United Nations

2008, p. 6). Planning for economic growth at the regional level can be considered as a part of an 'investment plan', which according to Galbraith (1962) reflects 'decisions on how best to employ scare capital resources' (p. 52). It is common practice for regions to develop a strategic plan with objectives that are focused on targeted development outcomes (Stimson et al. 2006, p. 100). Plans draw on resources to achieve goals or attempt to realise predetermined results. Hence, there is a need, as Barca et al. (2012) note, for 'a clear *ex ante* definition of the aims and intended outcomes in terms of well-being and socioeconomic progress of the interventions and a clear selection of the appropriate outcome indicators, necessary to assess whether the goals and outcomes have been reached' (p. 148).[17] The objective and outcomes in Sects. 4.3 and 4.4 can be used as guidelines in developing statewide strategies of economic development.

Webber (1963) defines planning as a 'rather special way of deciding which specific goals are to be pursued and which specific actions are to be taken' (p. 320). A planning model, therefore, incorporates 'a desirable unitary end state, a portrait of the future developed by using specific analytical and implementing tools and supported by a bundle of value propositions which tend to legitimise as well as constrain the activity of planning' (Galloway and Mahayni 1977, p. 69). The framework articulated in this chapter establishes goals, determines alternative policies and assembles strategies.[18]

An important element of regional development, according to Stimson et al. (2006), is the preparation of policies that describe the desired future directions of development in a region (p. 99). Thirlwall (1994) argues that 'the overriding object of a planned development programme is to incorporate society's choice of goals and to allocate resources to meet these goals' (p. 172). The decision-making process described in this chapter includes a desirable unitary end state, approximated by a predetermined level of national income and a minimum degree of regional inequalities, which reflects, at least to a certain extent, the choices of society. By setting realistic targets and applying the process proposed in this chapter, a democratic aspect is added in the process of economic planning, provided that agents realise the need to accept a relatively high level of regional disparities (or a low level of total output) for a given period of time. It is also an effective and sustainable funding measure and contributes in underpinning the legitimacy and accountability of regional policy. In other words, it can be used as a proper understanding of what regional policy is and how it operates. Such points, inevitably, bring the issue of *evaluating* regional policies into consideration.

The process of evaluating regional policy and regional planning are interrelated. Regional planning should have overarching goals, as well as clearly defined principles, responsibilities, procedures and instruments, elements which give scope for evaluating regional policies. Evaluating regional policy can be considered as a 'tool' for improving policy-making and the effectiveness of regional policy.[19] Hooghe (1996) argues that 'policy is made in turf battles between[...]bureaucracies, such that policy-makers are often far more concerned with enhancing their power than with solving a problem. So policies tend to be ineffective, incremental, and incoherent' (p. 93). Moreover, in several methods of evaluating regional policy, there is a lack of tangible criteria for assessing whether a specific measure of regional policy was successful or not. The approach developed in this chapter provides such criteria together with a method (indirect) for an (ex-post) evaluation of regional policy. Suppose that at an initial time, $t = t_0$, a given level of $G_{i,j}$ prevails. Assume further that $G_{i,j}$ is considered to be 'unacceptable' by society. Policy-makers, reflecting society's choice, decide to reduce the gap in regional incomes to an 'accepted' level. Assume that a certain level of regional inequalities corresponds to a given level of national income, which is accepted from efficiency point of view. Obviously, if $Y_N(t_0) - Y_N(T) < 0$ and $G_{i,j}(t_0) - G_{i,j}(T) > 0$, then it might be argued that regional policy was successful. In other words, these conditions can be considered as an attempt to measure the degree of precision in expressed objectives. If the level of national income is not the one expected from efficiency point of view, then a different allocation policy can be applied. Having knowledge on the structural characteristics of each region, it is possible to estimate the particular time at which policy should be changed in order to achieve specific targets. The approach outlined in this chapter allows alternative courses of action to be evaluated. In this way, it is possible to see where and when the policy was successful or not, increasing the ability of policy-makers to make optimal decisions. It is a process of continuously reviewing regional policies, which provides valuable information.

Objectives according to Perloff (1968) are 'conditional and dynamic and the priority given to them may be expected to change through time' (p. 154). The allocation policies, as a strategy of regional development, should be of dynamic and flexible nature, and regional economic plans should be adapted accordingly. By altering the weights attached to aims, the approach proposed in this chapter is a 'rolling' plan in which constraints for new investment programmes might be revised periodically to reflect information generated during the previous period (Marglin 1967).

It should be noted, however, that there is a tendency for civic leaders to confuse a particular development tool or project with a comprehensive strategy plan (Stimson et al. 2006). Stewart and Streeten (1976) note that '*strategy* is often used to describe a set of policies towards development, but the term covers not only the policies but also the objectives they are intended to fulfil. Thus strategies differ because objectives differ as well as because proposed policies differ [...] *objectives* to describe ends, and *programmes* to describe the *set of policies* designed to achieve the objectives' (p. 388) [emphasis in the original].

With respect to the process of regional planning, the words of Hall (1974) must be kept in mind: 'Planning in practice, however well managed, is therefore a long way from the tidy sequence of the theorists. It involves conflicts of values which cannot be fully resolved by rational discussion or by calculation; the clash of organised pressure groups and the defence of vested interests; and the inevitable confusions that arise from the complex interrelationships between decisions at different levels and at different scales, at different points in time' (p. 293).

To conclude this section, it is hoped that enough guidance on the matters is given in this chapter to make the economic analysis and policy intelligible to the reader who has worked through the previous chapters.

4.6 Conclusion

While Okun (1975) claims that 'the conflict between equality and economic efficiency is inescapable' (p. 120), the analysis in this chapter has shown that this is not so. Using an explicit regional context and logical deductions, compatibility in the aims of regional policy is feasible by modifying the aim of 'regional equity' and attaching an appropriate weight to the objective function. Adjusting the value of this weight, according to the existing conditions and new circumstances, it is possible to construct a set of several objective functions and, by extension, a wide range of optimal allocation policies, which incorporate features from 'aggregate efficiency' together with elements of 'regional equity'. The set of policies developed in this chapter do not represent a case of holding back productive regions in order to promote activity in lagging regions of the economy. They aim to ensure that lagging regions are able to realise their full economic potential and contribute to the growth of the economy as a whole. In other words, the 'policy-making machinery' proposed in this chapter ensures a high rate of growth for the economy as a whole and provides protection to lagging regions.

There is, however, another issue. As explicitly stated, the approach developed in this study refers to the short run. How, then is it possible to tackle development problems, issues in which, normally, a long-run perspective is attached? It would be more appropriate to claim that the approach in this study sets or creates the conditions for long-run development.

Development policy tries to provide solutions to specific problems, such as growth, structural change and income distribution. The approach developed in this chapter provides some insights or tackles simultaneously with these three issues. To be more concrete, a critical parameter of the model, namely, the growth rate of a region, is influenced by the allocation policy that government applies, which, in turn, influences the distribution of income across spatial units. Incorporating a sectoral perspective in the model of regional allocation of investment tackles with issues of structural change, if a switch in the sectoral composition in a region occurs as a result of the allocation policies applied. As implied in Sect. 4.4, the sectoral approach allows flexibility for investing in different regions and sectors over a long-run programming period, that is, a 'combination' of regional and sectoral policy: a strategy of polycentric regional development.

Regional policy takes place in a background of major economic crisis in the face of structural changes, rapid technological change, enhanced international competition and globalisation. The crisis, overall, has negative impacts on growth, public finances, increasing unemployment and poverty. This demands a set of ambitious policy answers to the problems of the future. The question as to which of these broad policy implications should be brought out in practice depends not merely on the specialised knowledge of planners and economists but ultimately on the far-sighted wisdom of policy-makers.

This chapter developed the 'strategic architecture of regional policy', namely, a model that simultaneously overcomes policy conflicts in both the regional and the sectoral level, which can be used as an 'overall' framework for development planning and evaluation of individual projects in conjunction with policy choices into a unified decision system.

Notes

1. Just how good a criterion of well-being real income per head is has been questioned, but it is generally accepted as significant when comparing societies of similar aspirations and roughly similar productive structures (Ford 1966, p. 24).
2. It is also possible to consider other proxies, such as average income, a percentage of national income, (e.g. 1% of aggregate growth per 5% reduction in interregional inequalities). Adopting such proxies, however, does not alter the main conclusions.
3. A term proposed by Mendez and Bachtler (2015).
4. The value of this weight depends on the structural characterises in each region. Interregional migration, for example, may be reflected in the weight. Suppose, for example, that as a result form investing in an initially rich region, labour migrates from the poor region. In a subsequent period, the weight may change, depending on the outcome of the previous period.
5. This is a methodological issue and the result of a complex process of interaction among regional, national authorities, politicians, planners, administrators, various (formal and informal) community groups, opinion polls and public hearings.
6. Recollect that $(v_1 + v_2) > 0$ implies $(v_1 - v_2) - (v_1 + v_2) < 0$.
7. A similar situation can be detected if $\gamma_1 > \gamma_2$ and $v_1 < v_2$. Implicit here is the Pareto's second theorem: real per capita growth is a necessary prerequisite for a reduction in income inequality. See also McLure (2013).
8. An argument put forward by Lucas (1976).
9. Previously article 159 TEC.
10. Such strategy is similar to that proposed by Rawls (1972).
11. These weights can be applicable to actual regional policies and can be devised in several ways as to reflect the existing conditions in each region and the policy followed (spatial targeting). Consider, for example, the Objective 1 regions, that is, regions with GDP per head below 75% of the EU average at the time of eligibility for funding. The weight may reflect the focus of policy, for example, improving infrastructure so as to help create the conditions for sustained growth or regions where development had occurred in the past but which were left with declining industries, sparsely populated regions in which the priority is to establish competitive businesses partly in order to maintain population.
12. It is possible to apply policies of partial allocation. In this case, $\beta_i \in]0\,1[$ and $\beta_i = f(\varphi_i)$, with $f > 0$. The optimal solution, therefore, is $\beta_j^* \to 1$ and $\beta_i^* \to 0, \forall i \neq j$.

13. This implies that the parameters involved must all be such as to relate the sectoral activities to some central index of macroeconomic activity. National income can be considered as a sufficient index.
14. In the absence of well-organised markets, for example, planning may provide quantity signals in order to give agents some idea about the extent of the future demand for their products. This has been alleged as a rationalisation for French Planning (Malinvaud 1965).
15. Planning, according to Stewart (1973), is the control of externalities.
16. Regional planning is a particular form of public planning action, embracing both economic and physical planning, applied at the sub-national but supra-urban scale. In Great Britain, for example, regional planning owes its origins to two quite separate conceptions: the problem of creating a better physical environment in the conurbations and the problem of regions suffering serious economic problems (Goodall 1987).
17. Indeed, several member states (and regions) of the EU find it difficult to formulate well-defined specific goals, partly to maintain flexibility in implementation (Mendez and Bachtler 2015). Applying the model developed in the previous section helps planners and decision-makers to identify the development and investment needs, to set up a programming process, investigate alternatives and choose the optimum and acceptable strategy for regional development.
18. Although these two definitions refer to physical planning (land use) a parallel set of arguments can be used for regional economic planning.
19. Cohesion Policy, for example, is not just a catalyst for evaluation but also a vehicle for disseminating standards and methods across the EU. Moreover, the recent austerity and budget restrictions have led to an increased demand for accountability about the results of regional policy and instruments (Polverari et al. 2015). For a more detailed analysis, see Huber (2006).

References

Ahluwalia, M., & Chenery, H. (1974). The Economic Framework. In H. Chenery (Ed.), *Redistribution with Growth* (pp. 38–51). Oxford: Oxford University Press.

Arrow, K. (1979). The Trade-Off Between Growth and Equity. In H. Greenfield et al. (Eds.), *Theory for Economic Efficiency: Essays in Honour of Abba P. Lerner*. Cambridge, MA: MIT Press.

Bachtler, J., Wishlade, F., & Yuill, D. (2003). *Regional Policies After 2006: Complementary or Conflict?* (European Policy Research Paper Number 51). European Policies Research Centre, University of Strathclyde.

Baldassari, M., & Piga, G. (1996). Distributive Equity and Economic Efficiency: Trade-Off and Synergy. In M. Baldassari, P. Luigi, & E. Phelps (Eds.), *Equity, Efficiency and Growth* (pp. 257–274). London: Macmillan Press.

Barca, F., McCann, P., & Rodríguez-Pose, A. (2012). The Case for Regional Development International: Place-Based Versus Place-Neutral Approaches. *Journal of Regional Science, 52*(1), 134–152.

Blakely, E. (1994). *Planning Local Economic Development: Theory and Practise* (2nd ed.). Thousand Oaks: Sage Publications.

Chenery, H., & Raduchel, W. (1971). Substitution in Planning Models. In H. Chenery (Ed.), *Studies in Development Planning* (pp. 29–47). Cambridge, MA: Harvard University Press.

Chinitz, B. (1966). Appropriate Goals for Regional Economic Policy. *Urban Studies, 3*(1), 1–7.

Cullingworth, B., & Nadin, V. (2006). *Town and Country Planning in the UK* (14th ed.). London: Routledge.

Dakin, J. (1963). An Evaluation of the "Choice" Theory of Planning. *Journal of the American Institute of Planners, 29*(1), 19–27.

Dasgupta, A., & Hagger, A. (1971). *The Objectives of Macro-Economic Policy*. London: Macmillan.

De Melo, J. Dervis, K., & Robinson, S. (1978). *Planning Models and Development Policy: Computable General Equilibrium Models* (Discussion Paper No. 79). Woodrow Wilson School, Princeton University.

Evans, A. (1974). Economics and Planning. In J. Forbes (Ed.), *Studies in Social Science and Planning*. New York: John Wiley.

Ford, A. (1966). Economic Growth: A Theoretical Outline. In W. Birmingham & A. Ford (Eds.), *Planning and Growth in Rich and Poor Countries* (pp. 15–61). London: George Allen and Unwin.

Galbraith, J. (1962). *Economic Development in Perspective*. New York: Fawcett Publications.

Galloway, T., & Mahayni, R. (1977). Planning Theory in Retrospect: The Process of Paradigm Change. *Journal of the American Planning Association, 43*(1), 62–70.

Gardiner, B., Martin, R., Sunley, P., & Tayler, P. (2013). Spatially Unbalanced Growth in the British Economy. *Journal of Economic Geography, 13*(6), 889–928.

Glasson, J. (1992). The Fall and Rise of Regional Planning in the Economically Advanced Nations. *Urban Studies, 29*(3/4), 505–531.

Goodall, B. (1987). *Dictionary of Human Geography*. New York: Penguin.

Hall, P. (1974). *Urban and Regional Planning*. London: Pelican Books.

Haveman, R. (1977). On Evaluating the Regional Impact of Public Policy. In E. Smith (Ed.), *Explorations in Economic Research: New Directions in Federal Economic Development Programs, 4*(3), 429–444, National Bureau of Economic Research.

Hooghe, L. (1996). *Cohesion Policy and European Integration*. Oxford: Oxford University Press.

House, J. (1973). Geographers, Decision Takers and Policy Makers. In M. Chisholm & B. Rodgers (Eds.), *Studies in Human Geography* (pp. 272–305). London: Heinemann.

Huber, W. (2006). Evaluation of the EU Cohesion Policy: Window-Dressing, Formal Exercise of Coordinated Learning Process? *Regional Studies, 40*(2), 277–280.

Isard, W. (1956). Regional Science and the Concept of Region. *Papers in Regional Science, 2*, 1–9.

Kenworthy, L. (1995). Equality and Efficiency: The Illusory Trade-Off. *European Journal of Political Research, 27*, 225–254.

Killick, T. (1976). The Possibilities of Development Planning. *Oxford Economic Papers, 28*(2), 161–184.

Lucas, R. (1976). Econometric Policy Evaluation: A Critique. In A. Whiting (Ed.), *The Philips Curve and Labour Markets* (pp. 19–46). Amsterdam: North-Holland.

Malinvaud, E. (1965). Interest Rates and the Allocation of Resources. In F. Hahn & F. Brechling (Eds.), *The Theory of Interest Rates*. London: Macmillan.

Marglin, S. (1967). *Public Investment Criteria*. London: Allen and Unwin.

Martin, R. (2008). National Growth Versus Regional Equality? A Cautionary Note on the New Trade-Off Thinking in Regional Policy Discourse. *Regional Science Policy and Practice, 1*(1), 3–13.

McLure, M. (2013). A. C. Pigou's Rejection of Pareto's Law. *Cambridge Journal of Economics, 37*(4), 775–789.

Mendez, C., & Bachtler, J. (2015). *Prospects for Cohesion Policy in 2014–20 and Beyond: Progress with Programming and Reflections on the Future* (European Policy Research Paper Number 14). European Policies Research Centre, University of Strathclyde.

Michel, P., Pestieau, P., & Thisse, J. (1983). Regional Allocation of Investment with Distribute Objectives. *Journal of Regional Science, 23*(2), 199–209.

Moore, T. (1978). Why Allow Planners to Do What They Do? A Justification from Economic Theory. *Journal of American Institute of Planners, 44*(4), 387–398.

Okun, A. (1975). *Equality and Efficiency: The Big Trade-Off*. Washington, DC: The Brookings Institution.

Osberg, L. (1995). The Equity/Efficiency Trade-Off in Retrospect. *Canadian Business Economics, 3*(3), 5–20.

Pen, J. (1965). *Modern Economics*. London: Pelican.

Perloff, H. (1968). Key Features of Regional Planning. *Journal of the American Institute of Planners, 34*(3), 153–159.

Polverari, L., Bachtler, J., & van der Zwet, A. (2015). *Evaluating the Effectiveness of Regional Policy* (European Policy Research Paper No. 91). University of Strathclyde.

Rawls, J. (1972). *A Theory of Justice*. Oxford: Clarendon Press.

Regulation (EEC) No 2052/88 of June 1988 on the Tasks of Structural Funds and Their Effectiveness and on Coordination of Their Activity Between Themselves and with the Operation of the European Investment Bank and Other Existing Financial Instruments, *Official Journal of the European Community* No. L 185/9 of 15 July 1988.

Reiner, T. (1965). Sub-National and National Planning: Decision Criteria. *Papers in Regional Science, 14*, 107–136.

Sen, A. (1975). *Employment, Technology and Development*. Oxford: Clarendon Press.

Stewart, M. (1973). Markets, Choice and Urban Planning. *Town Planning Review, 44*(3), 203–220.

Stewart, F., & Streeten, P. (1976). New Strategies for Development: Poverty, Income Distribution, and Growth. *Oxford Economic Papers, 28*(3), 381–405.

Stimson, R., Stough, R., & Roberts, B. (2006). *Regional Economic Development: Analysis and Planning Strategy*. Berlin: Springer.

Thirlwall, A. (1994). *Growth and Development* (5th ed.). London: Macmillan.

Todaro, M. (1971). *Development Planning: Methods and Models*. Oxford: Oxford University Press.

Trevo, H. (1989). A Micro-Level Approach to the Analysis of the Displacement Effects of Regional Incentive Policy: The Case of Finland. *Regional Studies, 23*(6), 511–521.

United Nations. (2008). *Spatial Planning: Key Instrument for Development and Effective Governance*. Geneva: United Nations.

Vanhove, N., & Klaasen, L. (1980). *Regional Policy: A European Approach*. Aldershot: Avebury.

Walker, B. (1981). *Welfare Economics and Urban Problems*. London: Hutchinson.

Waterstone, A. (1966). *Development Planning: Lessons of Experience*. London: Oxford University Press.

Webber, M. (1963). The Prospects for Policy Planning. In L. Duhl (Ed.), *The Urban Condition* (pp. 319–330). New York: Basic Books.

Wishlade, F., & Michie, R. (2009). *Pandora's Box and the Delphic Oracle: EU Cohesion Policy and State Aid Compliance* (European Policies Research Centre, IQ-Net Thematic Paper No. 24(2)). University of Strathclyde.

CHAPTER 5

Conclusion

Abstract The aims of regional policy are not entirely clarified and may contradict each other. A conflict in the aims of regional policy is considered to be unavoidable. The primary contribution of this study is to provide a method to construct regional (investment) policies, which overcome the trade-off in the aims of regional policy. This chapter presents a conclusion by providing an overall summary of the thesis developed in this study and suggests avenues for future research on 'conflict-resolution' in regional policy.

Keywords Regional policy • Development strategy • Future research

JEL Classification R10

Governments and policy-makers often face difficulties in the design and/or implementation of regional policies. This stems from the fact that the aims of regional policy are not entirely clarified and may contradict each other. Clarifying the objectives of regional policy is only a first step. One needs to look for optimal policies to achieve those objectives. Contemporary policy-making is concentrated rather on 'aggregate efficiency' since the conflict in aims is considered to be unavoidable. But, isn't it time to abandon this simplistic interpretation? It seems that there is wish to change in the air.

S. Alexiadis, *The Dilemma of Regional Policy*,
https://doi.org/10.1007/978-3-319-68900-5_5

The primary contribution of this study has been to provide a set of 'resource-efficient' regional policies using some of the key concepts relating to OCT. This approach, however, is by nature of restrictive character. Apart from high uncertainty and incomplete information, such exercise is, by its very nature, limited; it simplifies a complex reality. For example, it is almost an article of faith of regional economics that production is characterised by substantial localisation and urbanisation economies. Spatial externalities justify policy intervention and planning, especially, from an economic efficiency point of view. Incorporating spatial externalities, economies of scale and other sources of non-convexities into a model of regional allocation of investment opens up a promising avenue for future research.

If one considers only interregional inequality, other aspects, such as the distribution of income within a region, are ignored. It is not all clear that policies which benefit depressed regions also benefit poor people in these regions. In other words, it is quite possible that policies reducing interregional inequalities increase inequalities *within* regions. Interregional inequalities are as undesirable as intraregional inequalities. Nevertheless, the interaction between interregional and intraregional inequalities is another important area for future research.

This study puts primary focus on the process of capital accumulation. It is generally recognised, however, that this process cannot continue indefinitely; eventually, the rate of growth is conditioned by the quality of the labour force and other fixed factors. Moreover, the assumption of proportionality in output-capital ratios implies absence of any technological progress. From this perspective, the analysis in this study refers to short-run policies. In the long run everything changes. Improvements in technology take place and contribute to a reduction in regional inequalities. Developing allocation policies that explicitly incorporate technology is another important area for future research.

Much further work will be needed to clarify and carry further the values that should be attached to the aims of regional policy. What relative weights should be attached to 'regional equity'? In addition, there is the question of how to define a 'tolerable' level of interregional disparities. To what extent is society willing to tolerate regional disparities? There are no analytical methods which permit consistent evaluation of such factors. Until such methods are developed, the solution of this problem must be achieved by statistical system analysis, logical arguments, experience and continuous observation.

The current economic crisis demands a set of ambitious policy answers to the problems of the future. Future work on regional policy calls for use of more complex development plans and realistic policy models. Thinking towards the future is an essential precondition for investigating where policies are necessary and how they should be shaped. The contribution of the analysis would be to indicate that investment policies which overcome the trade-off in the aims of regional policy are feasible. An allocation policy that maximises national income without exceeding a predetermined 'gap' in regional incomes is a rational way to tackle with the dilemma of regional policy, at least in the short run. The important point to grasp is that this study offers a set of optimal allocation policies, enabling policy-makers to achieve simultaneously the aims of 'aggregate efficiency' and 'regional equity'. Although this is a difficult and ambitious task, the analysis in this study has shown that it is feasible under certain conditions; a point that should be taken into account by policy-makers when they design investment policies for regions and development projects. The approach in this study explicitly integrates the trade-off in the aims of regional policy improving resource allocation between regions and eventually reducing inconsistencies in decision-making.

Application of the model discussed in this study constitutes a challenge for policy-makers and practitioners, in different sectors and at different geographical and administrative levels. Hence, there is a need to rethink the future direction of regional policies along the lines of the implementation of innovative and region-specific development strategies, based on the concept of optimality in decision-making.

Appendix

Maximising Total Consumption

Following a standard practice in macroeconomic modelling, consumption (C) is assumed to be proportional to income, implying that savings are also proportional to income: $C_N = \Upsilon_N - I_N$. Since, by definition $I_N \equiv S_N$, then $C_N = \Upsilon_N - S_N$; given that $S_N = s\Upsilon_N$, then $C_N = \Upsilon_N - s\Upsilon_N$ or $C_N = (1-s)\Upsilon_N$; consequently, $C_N = \sum_{i=1}^{n} C_i$ and $C_i = (1-s_i)\Upsilon_i$, $\forall i = 1,2$.

Population (P) is assumed growing at the exponential rate η and normalised to unity at $t=0$. Thus, $P = \mathrm{e}^{\eta t}$. Per capita consumption is then defined as $C/P = C\mathrm{e}^{-\eta t}$. The problem at hand is to maximise $\int_0^T (C/P)dt$ or $\int_0^T \mathrm{e}^{-\eta t}\left[(1-s_1)v_1K_1 + (1-s_2)v_2K_2\right]dt$ over a finite time period by choice of $\delta(t)$, subject to the constraints $\dot{K}_1 = \delta(\gamma_1K_1 + \gamma_2K_2)$ and $\dot{K}_2 = (1-\delta)(\gamma_1K_1 + \gamma_2K_2)$.

As a first step, the Hamiltonian function is specified:

$$H = \mathrm{e}^{-\eta t}\left[(1-s_1)v_1K_1 + (1-s_2)v_2K_2\right] + p_1\delta(\gamma_1K_1 + \gamma_2K_2) + p_2(1-\delta)(\gamma_1K_1 + \gamma_2K_2) \quad \text{(A1)}$$

Equation (A1) may be written in the alternate form:

$$H = \mathrm{e}^{-\eta t}(v_1K_1 + v_2K_2) + \left[\delta(p_1 + p_2) + p_2 - \mathrm{e}^{-\eta t}\right](\gamma_1K_1 + \gamma_2K_2) \quad \text{(A2)}$$

S. Alexiadis, *The Dilemma of Regional Policy*,
https://doi.org/10.1007/978-3-319-68900-5

Equation (A2) implies that the optimal path of the allocation parameter depends on the relation between *both* the regional differentials in v_i and γ_i. Since $\dot{p}_1 = -\partial H / \partial K_i \ \forall i = 1,2$, it follows that

$$\dot{p}_1 = -e^{-\eta t} v_1 - \left[\delta(p_1 - p_2) + p_2 - e^{-\eta t}\right]\gamma_1 \quad \text{(A3)}$$

$$\dot{p}_2 = -e^{-\eta t} v_2 - \left[\delta(p_1 - p_2) + p_2 - e^{-\eta t}\right]\gamma_2 \quad \text{(A4)}$$

Equations (A3) and (A4) can be written as

$$\dot{p}_1 = e^{-\eta t}(\gamma_1 - v_1) - \left[\delta(p_1 - p_2) + p_2\right]\gamma_1 \quad \text{(A5)}$$

$$\dot{p}_2 = e^{-\eta t}(\gamma_2 - v_2) - \left[\delta(p_1 - p_2) + p_2\right]\gamma_2 \quad \text{(A6)}$$

Equations (A5) and (A6) imply

$$\dot{p}_1 - \dot{p}_2 = -\left[\delta(p_1 - p_2) + p_2\right](\gamma_1 - \gamma_2) - e^{-\eta t}\left[(\gamma_1 + \gamma_2) - (v_1 - v_2)\right] \quad \text{(A7)}$$

$$p_1 - p_2 = \left[(\gamma_1 - \gamma_2)/\gamma_2\right]p_2 + \left(e^{-\eta t}/\eta\right)(\gamma_1/\gamma_2)(v_1 - v_2) \quad \text{(A8)}$$

$$\dot{p}_1(t)/\dot{p}_2(t) = \left[p_1(t) - p_1(T)\right]/\left[p_2(t) - p_2(T)\right] \quad \text{(A9)}$$

$$\left[p_1(t) - p_1(T)\right]/\left[p_2(t) - p_2(T)\right] = \gamma_1/\gamma_2 \quad \text{(A10)}$$

It follows, therefore, that

$$p_1(t) - p_2(t) = \left[(\gamma_1 - \gamma_2)/\gamma_2\right]p_2(t) + p_1(T) - (\gamma_1/\gamma_2)p_2(T) \quad \text{(A11)}$$

The objective function can be written as

$$\int_0^T e^{-\eta t}\left[b_1 K_1 - \gamma_1 K_1 + b_2 K_2 - \gamma_2 K_2\right]dt \quad \text{(A12)}$$

At $t=T$ $(e^{-\eta t}/\eta)(b_i-\gamma_i)K_i$. If $p_i(T)=\partial C(T)/\partial K_i(T)$, then $p_1(T)=(e^{-\eta t}/\eta)(b_1-\gamma_1)$ and $p_2(T)=(e^{-\eta t}/\eta)(b_2-\gamma_2)$.

Using Eq. (A8) gives

$$p_1(t)-p_2(t)=\left[(\gamma_1-\gamma_2)/\gamma_2\right]p_2(t)+\left(e^{-\eta t}/\eta\right)\left[(b_1-\gamma_1)-(\gamma_1/\gamma_2)(b_2-\gamma_2)\right] \quad \text{(A13)}$$

$$p_1(t)-p_2(t)=\left[(\gamma_1-\gamma_2)/\gamma_2\right]p_2(t)+\left(e^{-\eta t}/\eta\right)\left[(b_1-\gamma_1)-(\gamma_1 b_2)/\gamma_2+\gamma_1\right] \quad \text{(A14)}$$

$$p_1(t)-p_2(t)=\left[(\gamma_1-\gamma_2)/\gamma_2\right]p_2(t)+\left(e^{-\eta t}/\eta\right)\left[b_1-(\gamma_1/\gamma_2)b_2\right] \quad \text{(A15)}$$

$$p_1(t)-p_2(t)=\left[(\gamma_1-\gamma_2)/\gamma_2\right]p_2(t)+\left(e^{-\eta t}/\eta\right)\left[(v_1\gamma_2-\gamma_1 v_2)/\gamma_2\right] \quad \text{(A16)}$$

In steady-state $\gamma_1=\gamma_2$, hence

$$p_1-p_2=\left[(\gamma_1-\gamma_2)/\gamma_2\right]p_2+\left(e^{-\eta t}/\eta\right)(\gamma_1/\gamma_2)(v_1-v_2) \quad \text{(A17)}$$

This expression indicates that the optimal allocation depends on the relation between γ_i and v_i. The optimal time path can be specified as follows. If $\gamma_1-\gamma_2>0$ and $v_2-v_2>0$, then the allocation parameter remains unchanged $\forall t\in[0\ldots T]$. Given that $\Delta\gamma_{1,2}>0$ and $\Delta v_{2,2}>0$, by assumption, $\delta^*(t)=1$ at $0\leq t\leq T$. A negative relation between $\Delta\gamma_{1,2}$ and $\Delta v_{1,2}$ implies a switch in δ. If $\gamma_1-\gamma_2>0$ and $v_2-v_2<0$, then $\delta^*(t)=0$ at $0\leq t\leq t_0$ and $\delta^*(t)=1$ at $t_0\leq t\leq T$, where t_0 is the switching time.

Setting $p_1-p_2=0$, yields

$$\left[(\gamma_1-\gamma_2)/\gamma_2\right]p_2=\left(e^{-\eta t}/\eta\right)(\gamma_1/\gamma_2)(v_1-v_2) \quad \text{(A18)}$$

Using Eq. (A18) it is possible to obtain an expression for the switching time. Solving for t gives $t_0=(1/\eta)\ln[(\gamma_1/\eta p_2)(v_1-v_2)/(\gamma_1-\gamma_2)]$. It follows that $\partial t_0/\partial\eta<0$; a condition which states that the switching time is a decreasing function of η. The optimal policy, therefore, is twofold: (a) before the switching time $(0\leq t<t_0)$, invest only in the region with the higher output/capital ratio, and (b) after the switching time $(t_0<t\leq T)$, invest only in the region of higher growth rate, where the switching time is a decreasing function of η.

Maximising income at a terminal time leads to switching from high growth regions to high output/capital ratio regions, while maximising per capita consumption over a given time period leads to a reverse switching from regions with high output/capital ratio to high-growth regions.

Index[1]

[1] Note: Page numbers followed by "n" refers to note.

S. Alexiadis, *The Dilemma of Regional Policy*,
https://doi.org/10.1007/978-3-319-68900-5